Proverbs 3:5

PRAISE FOR *BROKENNESS INTO ONENESS*

"Wow! Read this book and rejoice in the faithfulness of the God who is at the center of the story. You'll be glad you did."

—Steve Brown
pastor, author, speaker, seminary professor,
and founder/radio host for Key Life Ministries

Jesus loves you!

Brokenness *into* Oneness

Brokenness into Oneness

One Man's Journey from Hell to Heaven

ERIC WONG

WITH CHARLIE WINKELMAN

TATE PUBLISHING
AND ENTERPRISES, LLC

To Jonathan & Abby
& Titus et al,
May God bless & use
you to help many
with brokenness
of all kinds to ment
I love you.
Heb. 12:1-2
In Jesus' love,
Charlie
W.

This book is designed to provide accurate and authoritative information with regard to the subject matter covered. This information is given with the understanding that neither the author nor Tate Publishing, LLC is engaged in rendering legal, professional advice. Since the details of your situation are fact dependent, you should additionally seek the services of a competent professional.

The opinions expressed by the author are not necessarily those of Tate Publishing, LLC.

Published by Tate Publishing & Enterprises, LLC
127 E. Trade Center Terrace | Mustang, Oklahoma 73064 USA
1.888.361.9473 | www.tatepublishing.com

Tate Publishing is committed to excellence in the publishing industry. The company reflects the philosophy established by the founders, based on Psalm 68:11,
"The Lord gave the word and great was the company of those who published it."

Book design copyright © 2016 by Tate Publishing, LLC. All rights reserved.
Cover design by Matthew Winkelman and Samson Lim
Interior design by Shieldon Alcasid
Editor and coauthor Rev. Charlie Winkelman

Published in the United States of America

ISBN: 978-1-68319-023-3
1. Biography & Autobiography / Personal Memoirs
2. Biography & Autobiography / Religious
16.07.07

BROKENNESS INTO ONENESS is the story of Eric Wong's journey from the brokenness of a hellish life into oneness with his Savior, Jesus Christ. It will encourage all who struggle with similar challenges, and those who love them.

Eric with daughter, Erica

Eric Wong has survived the *brokenness* of childhood physical, verbal, and sexual abuse, a broken family, abandonment, the early death of loved ones, drug addiction, attempted suicide, HIV (for twenty-five years with no antiviral drugs!), life-threatening crippling injuries, chronic pain, sexual immorality, divorce, bipolar disorder, near bankruptcy, and demonic attack! He did so only by the grace of God through a dramatic conversion and ongoing growth into the *oneness* of a personal relationship with Jesus Christ. Today Eric has a bachelor's degree in social work, does independent electrical contracting, and serves the church as a youth worker, elder, and speaker. He resides in Jersey Shore, Pennsylvania, and has two grown children.

Charlie Winkelman is the pastor of a small Presbyterian church in Jersey Shore, Pennsylvania, a thirty-six-year youth ministry veteran, and Eric's friend for the past twenty-four years. He and his wife, Laura, have two grown children.

Contents

PART I

MY STORY

In part 1, I tell the story of how I became broken, tried to escape down various dead-end paths, and finally turned to Christ, who brought me through continuing trials into oneness with Himself and fruitful ministry with youth and others.

1

Brokenness and Oneness

I AM WRITING this book with the hope that whoever reads it will experience the transforming power and glory of God, through His Son Jesus Christ. This story shows God's grace as well as His ability to change us through the Holy Spirit and God's Word. With all my heart, my further hope is for God, not me, to be glorified. Any glory that may come my way in fact belongs only to Him, because of His work in my life and my adoption into His family.

The Characters

In my life there have been many people used by God as part of His teaching, each playing a significant role. I have used their real names only where given permission. I dedicate this book first to God through Jesus Christ, and second to the following people. The first person is my daughter, Erica, with whom I have been reunited. My love for her was restored when I rededicated my life to Christ in 1988 and has grown ever so powerful over the years. She is the sunshine of my life and is now a big part of it. God has used my love for her as a tool to teach me how to be a father.

When I was eleven or twelve, my uncle, Donald Sheets, brought me and my cousin to a youth retreat in Virginia. During this time, I was undergoing surgery on my hips due to a condition where my body was growing more quickly than my bone structure. There was a speaker who presented the gospel and gave an altar call (an invitation to accept Jesus as Savior and Lord). During this call, I prayed and asked God for healing, and also accepted Jesus. I felt His presence, and God planted a seed.

Following this, my parents were going through a nasty divorce, and God put a Christian friend in my life. Sherry Dalton was my youth leader at First Presbyterian Church in Quincy, Massachusetts, when I was twelve years old. She took me out for ice cream and presented the Gospel of Jesus Christ to me. In the midst of my brokenness from my parents' separation, God used her small act of kindness to help plant another seed for a very significant moment in my life many years later.

That moment came when I was twenty-eight, and God's seeds sprouted. I had hit a major bottom.[1] Remembering all the times I had been told about Jesus, as well as my experiences at my boyhood church, I found myself led to its doors. There I met Pastor Jeff Arnold. As he ministered to me, God took hold of me and showed me His immense love for me, and I once again invited Jesus Christ to be my Savior and Lord, this time with a much fuller understanding of what I was doing.

Even though I accepted the Lord, there was a great deal of work to be done regarding my behavior. At this point, God put a teacher in my life, Dr. Bob Brown, who ran a halfway house for recovering addicts. God hand-selected this man to work with me for the next four years, using him to continue to transform me, break me, and remold me during my beginning years as a dedicated Christian. Bob was unique—a big, tough man who also was a Christian who experienced God's awesome transforming power.

During this time of God's working transformation in me, God brought a young friend into my life named Matt Fuccillo. Matt was a student in the church youth group I was helping with as a volunteer. He was struggling. God used me to help redirect his life, and in the process, Matt and I became very good friends. God has used Matt's unswerving love and friendship, then and now, to help me grow.

---

[1] *Bottom* is a term often used with regard to addiction to describe a point in your life when you feel you cannot get any lower or you'll die.

Through my youth work at church, God put another teacher in my life. This man is Pastor Charlie Winkelman, a longtime friend from then till now. When we first met, it was about me helping him, but God has used Charlie to help me in many ways, loving me as a brother unconditionally. He spent many hours helping edit this book—a real labor of love considering my personal war against English grammar!

I would like to mention my friend Danny. Danny and I were raised in the same city. Danny, like me, had to endure brokenness, both before and after becoming a Christian. We ran together, and he has been my friend since I was fourteen. Through God's grace, he also accepted Jesus and has a powerful testimony. It is evident that God has transformed him as well.

I was ministered to and taught also by teachers who do not know me—pastors and Christian leaders including Charles Stanley, Chuck Swindol (a fellow Marine), Alistair Begg, Ravi Zacharias, James Dobson, and the late A.W. Tozer. I listened to the richness of God's word from these teachers on Christian radio during daunting hell nights. You could say the word of God preached by these men, in many cases, is what kept me from death over the past years.

And finally, I would like to mention my mother and father, who both died in 2012 (my mother of cancer and my father of an unknown illness) and went to be with the Lord. They both had many struggles in life, some of which caused deep hurt for me. But God used my mother's prayers that I would be saved, and her timely urging that I get back to church, to lead me back to Jesus, who saved me from all my brokenness through increasing oneness with Him. He even used my parents' deaths to bring about forgiveness and oneness within my family.

Before moving on to my story, let me make clear that anything I say regarding other people in my life is in no way intended to harm or be critical, but to show that they also were used as God's tools to mold me into the man I am today. All the people I interacted with had a part to play in God's plan for me today and into eternity.

The Story

The story I am about to tell is about my life before and after becoming a Christian. It's about my walk in life, choices I made, and the many things I had to overcome. But most of all it is about God's grace—His unearned favor and blessing.

Each of us has a story—a story of successes, accomplishments, achievements, and the brokenness that comes before and after. Mixed in with all of these experiences are the relationships that we build, relationships that rub hard and soft, helping form our deepest thoughts. And with these thoughts, our hearts grow. They feel love, hate, anger, frustration, and abandonment. Until we find our life's purpose or meaning, we also feel a sense of discontent and disconnection.

As I floated in this feeling of discontent and disconnection, I found ways to fill my heart with external things, things that for the moment brought a feeling of freedom. But these things did *not* free me—they put me in further bondage. As I grew, I thought I needed these things to help me escape from my heart's despair, because my life was that of a wandering child exposed to an onslaught of hell. Hell I got to know, but it was God and His heavenly life, which began here on earth, that freed me. But this has taken time.

The bondage that so entangled me came from what I was taught in making choices, these choices I made, and the direction of the evil in this world. My story involves addiction, drugs, violence, abuse, money, sex, disease, food, and spiritual warfare. These and my choices related to them produced the multiple negative conditions, diseases, behaviors, and feelings that I experienced. In all of this, before I came back to Christ, I was molded into a man who was mean, arrogant, hateful, dysfunctional, scared, angry, and out of control. Other than that, I was okay! I had to be remade, first by brokenness and then into oneness, the oneness that comes from God's holy hand through His Son Jesus Christ.

My story is also about how God's hand has performed miracles. Not only miracles of external healing, but the internal healing of my heart, mind, and soul. It is about Him slowly unlocking bonds—bonds of sin that so seized me. My experience with God has been like Marine boot camp, multiplied many times over. It has been occurring since 1988 when I rededicated my life to Jesus, although God was certainly involved in my life prior to that. God's relationship with me has warmed my heart, to free it from the past. In this freedom, God has given me a ministry, a ministry working with broken children and people, and this goes on to this day.

The Brokenness

We live in a world that challenges and strains every fiber in our being. These challenges start from the womb. As children are born, they shake, scream, and kick while coming out. Little do they know whether their life will be one of nurturing or pain. For some children it is pain, coming out only to be put in an environment that will treat them unfairly, and teach them to do the same to others.

Imagine a child being born to parents who are addicted to drugs and live in poverty. The child goes home after birth, only to be treated badly and pushed aside, abused and neglected. Life can be unfair.

As the child grows, he or she learns what living in hell is like—struggling to get a meal, clean clothes, or a safe environment. Children like this often live in a house that has many faces—faces with eyes ready to pop out of their heads, robots doing drugs or smoking on a stem.

The children inhale fumes from these crack pipes being smoked in the home. They see the use of pipes, needles, and other paraphernalia.

They learn to succumb to the arguments that come from addiction. They learn abuse and neglect. They learn to live in this confusing conundrum of hurtful people, places, and things.

Children find they have to hide from danger, sometimes in the closet, or they may sleep on a bed or floor, only to have a perpetrator who is laced on a chemical lying beside them with wicked intent. After an emotionally vexing night, they rise confused and daunted to seek for food. They find the refrigerator contains only morsels, baking soda, and possibly some sour milk. Oh, what suffering! Oh, how life can be unfair.

As children learn the ways of the family or group that has raised them, they often follow the same path. They find themselves doing the things they hate—using drugs, hitting the crack pipe, stealing, or selling their body to get resources to satisfy their addictions.

Deep in their heart sink all the things that happened to them, only to rise occasionally. As they grow up, they feel the pain from the experiences of their past, and possibly find that drugs can take it away temporarily. As life moves on, they mature, and get someone pregnant or get pregnant themselves. Then they raise their children in the same condition. Research has shown the high probability of a repeating cycle of drug use in families exposed to addiction. This happened to me in my life.

As the baby girl is born, she shakes, screams, and kicks while coming out. Little does she know whether her life will be one of nurturing or pain. For some children it is pain, coming out only to be put in an environment that will treat them unfairly, and teach them to do the same. Imagine a child being born to parents who are addicted and live in poverty. So the cycle repeats itself. Of course this is not always the case. Some grow up to be successful and rise above their upbringing. Although this sometimes happens, encapsulated in their hearts are the memories of their past.

Is this always the situation? No, not always. This is just one possibility. So you might have a child who is born into wealth and has all the amenities of life, a fine home, and parents that are well-to-do. But it seems as if the parents are never home, because they are career folks. Perhaps the mother is the biological parent in a new relationship, cohabitation. The child is given all that is needed. She goes to a private school and gets good grades. However, the parents find her angry and rebellious, and making bad choices regarding relationships with boyfriends. As she does not have a deep relationship with Mom, and especially with her biological dad, she acts out, and is put in detention frequently. Her parents see this as a small matter and spoil her with all the goods, to make her happy.

The real problem is that she needs Dad and Mom to spend *time* with her. As she grows, she learns how to date many boys. She makes connections with many, only to later hit bottom. After one of her encounters, she becomes sick—real sick. The parents schedule an appointment with a doctor. Two weeks later she is diagnosed with HIV, and she's pregnant. What now? Can the rich parents buy her health back for her? No. How is this young lady going to cope? She needs the love of her biological dad as well as her mom. What she needs even more is the love of Jesus! She expresses, "Why me? What have I done wrong?" Life is unfair.

I could write many more such tales from actual true stories that I have experienced firsthand. I have seen how the world can be unfair. Unfair because of the death of a girl I loved. Unfair because she was abused and ostracized due to HIV, and at the end died of AIDS. This was a disease back in the mid-eighties to early nineties that was considered a death sentence, a disease that brought fear to many communities. I had other friends who died from overdosing, friends who were stabbed to death, and friends who escaped, only to live to this day with pain in their heart from their past. And then there is me, still alive and not dead. Why me and not them?

In some cases I asked myself, given my circumstances of disease, addiction and abuse, which was better for me, life or death? When one knows Christ, death does not have such a sting, and God's word contains the answer. Is it fair that I lived and my friends died? I can state with confidence that I am alive only because of what Christ did for me, and my choosing to trust in Him! The end, for me, brought forth the blessing; that is, the end of the life I lived before I was reborn, when I accepted Christ. Life as I knew it ended, and then it began again as I joined in a relationship with Him. So does life really end? Speaking of this world, yes. However, living in the grace of God through Jesus, true life begins when we accept Him. It is our choice. God has a purpose for me, and how His purpose has come to fruition will be seen throughout the rest of my story.

There are many stories from the Bible that talk about the unfairness that comes from this world. Even God's chosen ones were not exempt from this unfairness. The Israelite patriarch Joseph was sold into slavery by his brothers, only to be blessed and eventually come to bless an entire nation. The Old Testament believer Job was extremely blessed by God, and then had everything taken from him, even his health. Today our world tries to deal with the storms of life through things like welfare, prescription drugs, and various social policies, none of which were available in the ancient world. But what the ancients did have, which are still available today, were the timeless remedies of prayer and a relationship with God. Those were the means by which Joseph, Job, and many others received blessing.

My story is one where I had to learn to depend on God's grace to rise above adversity, not by my own means, but by God leading me through brokenness into oneness. So without further ado, I present my story with hope that whoever reads this will make a choice to accept what Jesus Christ did on the cross, which breaks the bonds from our past and future sins, and brings forth freedom from now to eternity. Now join me on a journey as you read this book, a journey that has challenged me as I have reflected with my whole being on the seasons of my life.

2

Becoming Broken

And God said, "Let there be light," and there was
light. And God saw that the light was good; and
God separated the light from the darkness.

—Genesis 1:3–4

Now the word of the Lord came to me saying,
"Before I formed you in the womb I knew you, and
before you were born I consecrated you;"

—Jeremiah 1:4–5

In the Beginning

I WAS BORN on October 25, 1959. My father was native-
born Chinese, and my mother was American-born

German-Irish from Virginia. I think it is important to point out I was born after the Korean War and during the Vietnam War. This paints a picture regarding the cultural atmosphere, and how people viewed the Chinese, as well as interracial marriages.

My parents, my older sister Donna, my younger brother Neal, and I lived in Quincy, Massachusetts. We lived in a house on Federal Avenue, at the lower end. Behind the house was a railroad. This was fertile ground for my childhood imagination. It was as if there was this jungle, which needed to be explored. The trees were tall, the sewers deep, and the lumber yard adjacent to the tracks had mountains of wood that needed to be climbed. Needless to say this also presented many opportunities to get into trouble. We used to put nails on the rails to flatten them by the tons of weight from the train cars. We used these as boyhood weapons of war to throw at one another. Looking down the railroad tracks, they seemed to go for miles off into the horizon. We would jump the trains and go a distance into this horizon, believing we were in another place. Further down the tracks were hills. Thinking I was a great explorer, I would climb them searching for fossils and buried treasure. This was before the demise of my family through the divorce of my parents.

The lumber yard with the mountain of wood had a large lot. Here the neighborhood kids and I would team up to become great hockey players, like Boston's Bobby Orr and

Derek Sanderson. We would play for hours. But there was another place, which was not as kid-like, down at the end of Federal Avenue, a friend's house where a dark shadow lingered. A place where I would one day experience the ongoing use of drugs and alcohol. A place where the family had troubles, as well as experiences of abuse, "the house at the end of Federal Ave."

Beside the house was a beat up old '55 Chevy. A friend and I would sit in this car fantasizing great driving adventures. In the evening real cars would awaken, cars driven by a gang of older kids. In front of the house we would watch races, which went on up and down the road. Eventually the cops would come and chase them. After this happened, you would hear a loud voice from the front door, my friend's alcoholic father calling his children in, and it is sad what would happen next. The house down the road on the left was where I escaped from the pain I had, and shared it with the pain my friend had, by drinking and doing drugs during the weeks I was not in Boston. This is where I eventually joined the neighborhood gang, lived the life and learned the attitudes that accompany this lifestyle after my parents' divorce.

Quincy was predominantly Italian and Irish families. You could say that our family was somewhat normal. However, being Chinese did not make things easy, as a society impacted by the Vietnam War used labels like "Chink" and "Commie." We fit in like forcing a puzzle piece into the wrong spot. In the beginning I did not understand, but my father did. As I grew up, I would come to know what my father knew, that as a minority I must fight to stand my ground, fight no matter what it takes. This is what I learned to do—fight. And I learned something else—how to be a chameleon. More on that later.

My father was raised in Canton, China. He and his family were aristocrats. But having a title was not to their advantage because of communism. Everything his family owned was taken, and my father and his dad had to flee. They escaped to Hong Kong where they bought tickets to catch a freighter to San Francisco. My grandmother stayed, and it is sad to say, things were done to her that I will not mention. Eventually she was able to come over to America when I was young.

Alone with his father and disconnected from everything they knew, my father had to face a new culture and yet another form of prejudice, in the place of hoped-for sanctuary. When they arrived in San Francisco, they started to find odd jobs to survive. When they had saved enough money, they moved to Boston. They found a stable place to work and live in Chinatown. While living in Chinatown, my father met a man named Beverly Sheets and his wife, Francis. Beverly Sheets was the brother of my mother, Ruth.

My mother was raised in Staunton, Virginia, on a farm in the Shenandoah Valley. She was raised near a small town called Springhill and attended Springhill Presbyterian Church. Later, after Mom moved to Boston, married my dad, and had Donna, me, and Neal, Dad would send us down to Springhill every summer. We stayed at my aunt's house, which was located by a river.

On those summer mornings, I would wake up in a down-feather bed, a fresh cool country breeze flowing through the room from the windows on either side. Accompanying the breeze, the sweet smell of the dew and lilacs and honeysuckle that grew wild around the riverbanks would cause the sand in my eyes to fall off as I awakened. Another delightful smell in the morning was the smell of fresh coffee and eggs cooking. Every morning Wes, a friend of my grandparents who was like a grandfather to me, would be cooking breakfast. After eating breakfast, my cousins and I would wander and drift around the river, playing and getting into mischief. When we played, our imaginations used this river to take us around the world. We would capture copperheads and water moccasins that lived beside the river, and pretend we were great hunters. Neighborhood kids from Springhill would come down to join us in our hunting, and swim in the cool water, which relieved us from the heat of the day.

As the day drifted by toward evening, you would hear the cow bell call; this was the dinner bell. Dinner was always a delightful time and a special moment. All our relatives lived in the area, and we would all gather to eat dinner together.

Most times there were at least ten of us, with an adult table and a kids' table. Before each meal, Uncle Donny, a pastor, would say grace. After eating a country meal with all the fixings, the men would gather the dishes and take the task of washing them. Us kids would go outside and watch the transition of the day into night. We would lie on the warm grass looking into the sky with amazement, as the sun would set and millions of stars would open their eyes on the canvas of the night sky. As the moon rose, we did too, to sit in the chairs on the porch and reminisce.

Because we were over-energetic and could not sit long, we found that catching fireflies and putting them into jars kept us occupied. As the night drifted on, soon I would drift upstairs, flopping on the soft feather bed and falling asleep in anticipation of the next day's adventure. In most cases, this was a typical day at my aunt's house in my mom's hometown in Virginia. I have very fond memories of Springhill and my aunt's home, and life was good when we visited every summer.

It was during one of these summer vacations when I was eleven or twelve that Uncle Donny took me on a retreat where I heard an evangelist talk about Jesus and prayed to accept Him as my Savior. Loved by Jesus and enjoying boyhood adventures in God's beautiful creation with a close family, life didn't seem so unfair in Springhill! However, this would all end after my parents' divorce when I was twelve.

My mother, after growing up in Springhill, had gone through some trials from being involved with a very abusive man. In her late teens, she decided to run away to Boston to live, near her brother Beverly, who was in the Navy and stationed at the USS Constitution in Charlestown Navy Yard. My mother found a job working in a factory. Beverly introduced her to my father, who was working in a Laundromat, and they started dating. Apparently he once told her he was taking her to see the submarines come up in the Charles River. This naive country girl soon discovered that there are no submarines that come up in the Charles River.

After my parents met, they conceived my sister, Donna. My parents got married and moved to Germantown in Quincy, and pretty soon I came along. A couple years after my birth, my parents moved to 139 Federal Avenue, also in Quincy. This was where my brother, Neal, was born, and where we lived until the disintegration of my family. After my brother was born, things in the family began to change, and not for the better. My father favored my sister, while my mother favored my brother, leaving me as the "problem" middle child. This for me was the beginning of loss, degradation, abuse, and oppression.

Since my father was raised Chinese, I also was raised by the same methods. These methods involved being chastised frequently, as well as living in a very authoritarian environment. Not that I did not need both! But in some cases it was to the extremes and was not called for. (These methods were what I experienced, and I would not want to say that this was the case in all Chinese families.) As the "black sheep" of the family, I became the object of my father's anger, and my mother's frustration in dealing with him.

The Environment in Which We Lived

As I mentioned before, living in Quincy we were surrounded by two dominant cultures, Italian and Irish, during the Vietnam War. For a Chinese-American family, living in Quincy was like walking on eggshells. My sister and I experienced prejudice in the neighborhood, and as we attended school. We were the only two who were seen as different (especially because of the war), and therefore were treated differently. Not everyone did this; there was a church my mother, my sister, and I attended, and they were accepting and loving. This was my boyhood church, First Presbyterian Church of Quincy. I remember as a boy hearing Pastor Steve Brown preach on Sunday mornings. I felt a wonderful sense of comfort listening to him. Only later did I come to know this was the Holy Spirit speaking through his words. When I was older, this is where I truly and fully accepted Christ. Further in my story I will write about that awesome experience.

My experiences when I was being raised—ongoing chastisement and beatings by my father, and the oppression and degradation from people in the neighborhood and school—were things that I just accepted. But then something happened that brought feelings I had never felt before, feelings of rejection. When I was about nine, I was sexually molested by an older neighborhood boy. When my parents learned about this, they did nothing, out of fear of others in the neighborhood because the boy was Italian. I felt rejected by my own parents. This was the onset to suicidal thinking, which I tried a year or two later. Rejection was further exacerbated by my experience working for my father at his restaurant. My father wanted to teach me the value of a dollar, so he brought me to work with him. My job was to bus and wash dishes. This was not hard. What was hard was the cooks pinching me constantly while I worked. This left twisted bruises on my body. I was also paid less than the other boys who were working. But the really devastating storm on the horizon for my siblings and me was my parents' divorce. (For more on the abuse of my childhood and how I was helped to overcome the fall-out, see chapter 11.)

Things were not going right at home. My father was working long hours, my mother was upset, and there were many arguments late into the evenings. After my paternal grandfather died, things got even worse. My parents' divorce was inevitable. I was twelve when it happened. One morning I woke up to my mother crying downstairs in the kitchen. My father had not come home, and frantic phone calls and a visit to my paternal grandmother did not reveal his whereabouts. Eventually my mother discovered he had been with an old girlfriend, and our lives were turned upside down.

My life began to spiral downward, downward into an abyss it would take a lifetime to get out of, and then *only* by the grace of God through His Son Jesus Christ. As I spiraled down, I became one angry, violent young adolescent. I began punching walls and windows, and became a self-mutilator. I made weapons, weapons to kill my father in the event he would show his face. I blamed myself, my grades were affected, my relationships changed, and the utmost worst happened when I was moved to the ghetto of Boston's South End. This is where I found a new family, a family of drugs, alcohol, pornography, and an environment that would fuel the hate and contempt I had for my parents, as well as the world.

A New Environment

My mother had a hard time dealing with me. She was also having a hard time dealing with the divorce. So on weekends, school holidays, and summer vacations, she sent me to her brother's house in the South End of Boston, the ghetto. This is where I would learn about the heart of ghetto life culture, as well as my black and Hispanic extended family members. (My Uncle Beverly was married to an African-American woman, and many of my cousins were involved with Hispanic partners.) One other culture I would learn about was the drug culture. My aunt had fifteen children. They ranged in age from fourteen to thirty. I was about thirteen at the time. She also had live-ins, and even adopted a few children. One of these children was a young black man named Stanford who was a few years older than I was. He and I became close friends. He was the one I would drink and party with in the ghetto.

The ghetto of Boston's South End should not be mistaken for South Boston, the mostly Irish-American and somewhat nicer neighborhood across the highway. The South End was lined with four- and five-decker brownstone apartments on each block. The street I lived on was West Newton, number 123. In front of the homes were newly planted trees with pole lamps to light up the street. In the back were alleys lined with broken street lamps, and trash piled below them. On days when I walked down these alleys, to move from one block to another, I would see large rats scurrying, fighting for a morsel of food, surviving the jungle so to speak. In my experience living here, I also had to scurry to survive the jungle, but among people.

Down the road were O'Day and Blackstone Parks, where drug deals would go on, as well as gang or street fights. Enjoyable activities in the parks were "ghetto-ball" (no rules!) at the basketball courts and "Summer Thing" summer concerts sponsored by the community. During the day it was dangerous, but not as dangerous as it was at night. At night things happened, and night is when I learned to roam and party with my friends. Roaming and partying was not limited to the South End. Boston was also a new playground, where I got to know the streets and what predators to watch out for. My family had a reputation, so I had few worries.

While living at my aunt's house, I was dubbed with the name "Dummy." This name would tear into my mind and affect my emotions and every fiber of my being, even to the present day. Being called Dummy exacerbated my feelings about me being less than others and further reinforced the way my father spoke to and treated me. When working with my father at home, when my parents were still together, an ongoing comment from him was that I would never amount to anything and I was dumb. Hearing this from my father at a young age was awful; it tore and ripped like a saw into my soul and marrow. I could never meet his expectations, and this also I carried into my life as I grew older.

My daily life living in Boston consisted of me literally being treated like a dog. As the youngest, I learned to be a slave to all my cousins. I had to bow to everyone's beck and call. I was forced to go to the store at all hours of the day and evening. I had no life except the one dictated by my masters, and my night life.

While living in Boston, I learned what it was to work hard. My uncle owned a janitorial business. My role was to take trash down from apartment buildings. These buildings had many floors, and the trash stunk and was heavy. I also worked at cleaning. Each floor's hallway had to be mopped and waxed. Railings had to be dusted, and the carpets had to be vacuumed. At times I worked at demolishing and removing rubbish from apartments. These apartments had large refrigerators and heavy objects that had to be removed. They had rubbish that had piled up over time and smelled like death.

Working hard was made more difficult because I was not fed often. I had to depend on my masters to feed me. Many times I would go days without eating. I had to survive by scurrying around like a rat or dog. I learned to be a scavenger, picking from half-empty plates at pizza parlors, or checking out the trash can in our kitchen for morsels late in the evening. The refrigerator had a chain and lock on it.

One painful experience I remember was being upstairs in my cousins' room, after they just ordered from McDonalds. Sitting there like a dying dog, I watched my cousins eat their meal. One of my cousins knew I was hungry. Knowing this, he did nothing to help, but instead showed me how much less than a dog I was. We had two dogs. Having a whole burger left over, my cousin called one of the dogs over and gave the burger to the dog and not me. This just added to my feelings of worthlessness.

Eating was not the only thing I had to deal with. Sleep was also an issue. Sleeping in the late evening or early morning was a battle. Most evenings I had no bed to sleep on. I had to sleep on a hard chair or the floor. Sleeping on the floor was difficult because the house was infested with cockroaches that would crawl up on you. I also had to sleep lightly because of predators, the human type. My sleeping was never heavy. Dealing with all of this as well as feelings of abandonment from my parents, feelings of being worthless, and feelings of hunger, I found a cure—the family of drugs.

I was young, from age thirteen to seventeen, when I experienced this. Drugs adopted me into their family quickly and were readily available. These drugs were marijuana, downers, uppers, methamphetamine, acid, and cocaine. Each one helped me deal with different areas of my life that were negative. Today I know this was a lie from Satan. Marijuana and downers would suppress my feelings of worthlessness and help me sleep. Uppers and methamphetamine would suppress my feelings of hunger and help me work the long twelve- and fourteen-hour days. Acid was a recreational drug, which I would take when relaxing. By age seventeen I was a full-blown drug addict. One other area that "helped" me deal with my emotions was pornography. This also became an addiction. Pornography was highly available, and I experienced this viewing and reading porn starting at age thirteen.

Living in Quincy and Going to School

During the week, I would come back to Quincy and attend school. I also did drugs there, in most cases every day. By dealing drugs, I found I could support my habit. Stealing money from my mother also helped. I smoked pot every day, and my twelfth year of school I remember eating acid frequently. The feelings that I did not deal with through drug use came out in my relationships. I was violent, angry, and would not hesitate to harm someone. I was in frequent fights, which gave me a reputation. I was not approachable and held the world in contempt. I hated my parents. I remember being busted twice, once for drugs and the other time for trying to steal hub caps. My father intervened but then chastised me once more by telling me how much of a loser I was, in front of the police and the principal. I barely graduated from high school. However, the worst part was that neither one of my parents chose to attend my graduation, so I did not either.

In one sense, believe it or not, my view was that I was a good boy! I was good in sports at one time. I played baseball and football and basketball. My grades were good at one time. Nevertheless, I was a failure. It wasn't a conscious choice. It was a feeling I had from the lack of support from my parents. I always wanted a hero—my dad—but my hero never appeared. Although Dad never took that role, when

I attended church as a teenager, I was taught about another hero by my youth director, Sherry Dalton. That hero was Jesus Christ, Someone who would end up saving me when I grew older. But more on that later.

The Chameleon

Moving back and forth from Boston to Quincy, I learned to be a chameleon. I so much wanted to be accepted. I found ways to achieve this. On school days, when I lived in Quincy, I dressed like a tough guy. I wore a leather jacket or a long army trench coat, with jeans and a T-shirt. My shoes were army boots. I always rapped packs of Marlboro cigarettes in my sleeves.

When I lived in Boston, my attire consisted of jeans when I worked, but I dressed like my black cousins when we went partying, or clubbing. I wore double knit and polyester shirts with fancy designs. My pants were of the same fabric. My shoes were platforms, and I always had a pair of high top canvas Converse sneakers for basketball. When I was in Boston, I smoked Kools. Sneakers were a must because basketball was the sport. After work we would go down to Blackstone Park to play ghetto basketball.

For a large part of my life, I adapted to living in these two worlds. You could say I became very diverse. I had no identity because my identity changed as the environment did, like a chameleon. I wanted to have the right image.

Quincy First Presbyterian Church

First Presbyterian Church in Quincy where I attended was located on Franklin Street on a high hill. The church was often referred to as "the light on the hill." The pastor in my childhood days was Rev. Steve Brown, who now has a national radio program called "Key Life." The pastor when I came back to Christ was Rev. Roger Kvam. Both were godly men who taught the Bible faithfully and challenged the church to reach out with the love and Good News of Jesus Christ to others. This is where my experience with God started when I was young. My mother attended for a while, but she slowly faded away. My mother had a friend, Miss McDonald, who brought me to church.

Here I was taught about the Bible, and Jesus. I enjoyed church. Church was always a place that was away from the war zone, my home or Boston. For a period of time after my parents' divorce, I attended youth group. This is when I met Sherry Dalton. She knew I had problems. She met with my mom to talk to her, but to no avail.

Many times I would drink before youth group. Eventually I no longer attended. But this is the church where I would have a great revelation in the future when I realized I was broken.

3

Trying to Escape

Escape through the Marines

WHEN I TURNED seventeen, I was introduced to the armed forces. I thought that by joining the Marine Corps I could escape from the hell I lived in. So in 1977 my parents signed me over. On July 4 I found myself at Paris Island, South Carolina. Here I spent the next fourteen weeks learning about discipline. The Marine Corps was good for me. But it did not take from me the anger and contempt I held toward my parents, and for the world. What it did was teach me how to take my anger and use it to my advantage. They taught me how to fight, and fight well. I did well in boot camp. I lost weight and was in the best shape I have ever been.

Marine Corps boot camp is not for the faint of heart. The marines had three phases. All three phases consisted of breaking and rebuilding, breaking and rebuilding, and they did this well. My time in the Corps was a few years after Vietnam. There was still a degree of tension regarding Vietnam. Our drill instructors felt it would behoove them to make our conditioning one that would benefit us if the service were called back.

My senior drill instructor did double tours in Vietnam, as did one of my three other drill instructors. This being the case, I feel safe in saying they were nuts. But their experience added to our staying at a higher level of learning. They saw death, felt death, and saw the fallout of war. So they prepared us.

The first phase I would speculate was to weed out the ones that were not up to Marine Corps standards. They broke both our minds and bodies. This was done by a regimen of PT (physical training) and close order drill every day, and screaming. Added into the mix was the heat of the day, sweating, and sand flies. We did calisthenics at the hottest part of the day and push-ups on the hot asphalt until we got blisters. Close order drill entailed long hours of marching, learning cadence and commands, and staying at attention for long periods of time. During close order drill, we carried our M-16. This was not a heavy weapon, but our drill instructors made us hold it with two arms straight out in front of us for long periods, causing it to get very heavy.

PT consisted of a variety of calisthenics. One that brought us to our knees was called mountain climbers. This activity consisted of a combination of bends and thrusts along with being in a push-up position and kicking your knees into your chest. I remember at times we would do these up to an hour straight. As time went on, so did recruits, meaning they went on home!

In the beginning of the first phase, we started with seventy to eighty recruits but lost many along the way. There were always new faces of those who were setbacks, that is, those who failed at something in the second phase and were set back to the first phase. They were constantly weeding people out.

Days were long, sleep was minimal, and mornings came quick. We were in the racks at 9:00 p.m. and up in most cases between 3:00 and 4:00 a.m. Sometimes we had surprise inspections and visitors. The visitors were the green monsters, our drill instructors, coming into the barracks, waking us up, making us open our foot lockers, and scattering everything everywhere. Added to this, we had to find our gear in the mess and restore items in our foot lockers within a time limit, and not hours, but minutes. Other things happened that I will keep to myself out of total respect for the Corps.

The second phase was the rifle range, where we learned how to respect the power of and gain responsibility for the M-16, as well as how to fire it. I did very well on the rifle range and along with three other men from the Battalion was awarded an "Expert" badge. Although we were into the second phase and at the rifle range, we were still being conditioned by the regimen of PT and screaming.

The third phase was to fine tune the work they did on us. This was the testing phase, when we had to put into practice what we had learned, and were challenged in the amount of endurance we had acquired during the first two phases. We had to throw the grenade without hesitation, go through a major obstacle course, and go on a twenty-mile forced march with full seventy-lb. backpacks, followed by a simulated battle. There was a great deal more, but it would take too many pages to write. I think you get the picture. What I will talk about next is my feelings.

I am proud to be a former marine. The Marine Corps brought to the surface a sense of purpose. When I felt I could no longer go on, it showed me there was something greater that would push me: the human spirit. It is amazing how resilient God had made me. Looking back now, what I have learned most from this experience was that it was not my own spirit but rather the mighty hand of God that got me through the toughest boot camp, the Marine Corps boot camp.

Again there was the one ingredient that was not added— my parents attending my graduation. When I graduated, I saw all the other men's parents cheering for them, but there was no one cheering for me. This compounded my negative feelings for life.

Escape through More Drugs

The Marine Corps did not combat my drug problem. Still eating away at me like a cancer was the anger and contempt I had for life, and I continued to use drugs to escape these feelings. After graduation from boot camp, I was on reserve status, going on duty one weekend a month and two weeks in the summer.

During the times not on duty with the Corps, I had various jobs. The one that stuck was based on the electrical training I had received in high school. With this I was able to get my Journeyman's license. The license enabled me to get many jobs, only to lose them because of my addictions. Working and moving through life, I was living on the edge. The closer to death, the more exciting it was. Deep down inside I wanted to die.

Still hanging around the wrong groups of people, I was soon introduced to the needle, which was to be my downfall. One day, with a group of shooters (junkies), I went to the house of a dealer who was selling cocaine. One of the group members encouraged me to try shooting, so I obliged him. Wow! After shooting a ball (one shot of cocaine), I now become a slave to the needle and shooting coke.

I was just twenty years old. Soon my arm was laid waste with a track of holes. The many holes in my arm depicted the gaping hole in my heart. Two years went by, and I hit a bottom. I remember one day and evening staying up sticking a needle in my arm. Stuck to the spoon was cotton soaked in my blood. Stuck to my mind was the obsession to stick this needle in my arm again and again. With every jab came the rush, and with every rush, I milked my blood back into the syringe so I could inject it again and gain an additional rush. When the coke ran out, the next rush I would get would be the rush of major depression. This always accompanies a coke binge.

Finally coming to the light, and only through the prayers of my mother, I decided to be interviewed at a recovery home through the VA. But I came away from the interview thinking I was too young and that I could recover on my own. This did not work. When I was twenty-three, after eating a large amount of acid and other drugs, I tried to kill myself by overdosing with enough drugs and alcohol to kill an elephant. But I couldn't even do that right! For reasons known only to God, I didn't die but ended up in the hospital. And the scourge continued.

Escape through a Woman

Twenty-three, in denial, and wandering from one relationship to another, I found myself alone with my best friends: the needle, a spoon, and bags of coke. Unlike real friends, drugs do not talk back. But they hold you captive, and in a way, they *do* talk back. Echoing in the back of my mind was the call of the rush, which I had to endure each day. Waiting on pay day, I could hear the call of the rush get stronger. After spending all my money to feed my habit, I would find myself once again laid waste in a deep depression. Wasted and alone, this cycle went on. But a new chapter was about to begin. Through a mutual friend, I met the woman who would be the mother of my children.

Stacy was the only woman who tolerated me. She was young, good-looking, and street tough. She was seventeen and I was twenty-five when I met her. Although much younger, she and I had a lot in common. She was in need like I was, searching to find something to fill the holes in her heart put there by a very abusive upbringing. The relationship quickly got physical, and she moved in with me. We would soon conceive my daughter. Let me tell you the surrounding story.

Stacy, my friend Danny, and I were partying one evening. After drinking a gallon of vodka and doing a boat load of drugs (as usual), we went exploring to find the never-ending party. The exploration this time took us south from Boston all the way to Atlantic City, New Jersey! Stacy, Danny, and I are alive today only by a great miracle from God, because the events of this trip were very dangerous.

On the drunken drive down, I passed a semi on the right whose driver was trying to prevent that very maneuver. After arriving in Atlantic City, we got a room. Stacy and I gambled a little, but after awhile, it got boring. Danny chose to continue gambling and soon came running by, sweat dripping down his nose, with his Discover Card in hand screaming, "Aren't credit cards great! I can always get money when I am broke!" Stacy and I chose to go up to the room, where my daughter Erica was conceived.

The next day we had to be out of the room by 1:00 p.m. It was late afternoon when we left Atlantic City to drive back to Massachusetts. Thus the hell journey home began. I was extremely hungover. The car was an old Marquis the size of a tank, with a powerful engine. Little did we know that the tank's brakes were not so powerful.

Flying about eighty miles an hour over the bridge into New York City, I noticed in front of me that the cars were stopping for the toll. I pushed on the breaks, but there was no response! I looked back at Danny and screamed, "I lost the brakes!" Danny and Stacy buried their heads between their legs. Danny starting chanting, "We're gonna die!" As adrenaline cut through the alcoholic fog in my brain, I saw there was small passing lane to the right. Slamming the car to the right and downshifting, I rode the Jersey barrier on the right side, scraping the side of the car to slow us down. We flew through the toll booth with sparks flying but without hitting anything, and finally came to a stop seventy-five yards beyond it. Danny ran back to pay the toll, but the toll booth collector told him, "Go ahead. After what I saw, you don't need to pay!" Only by God's grace did the car limp back into Quincy seven hours later. This happened in April of 1987. Nine months later on February 3, 1988, Erica was born.

Continuing getting high and working for various electrical companies, I soon hit another bottom. I thought that having Stacy, and later Erica, in my life would help. But I began to realize their presence would not conquer my addiction. It just added additional stress, which caused me to abuse myself all the more, as well others who were in my circle of friends. I remember praying to God after each coke binge. I prayed for Him to take it away or let me die. As I continued on a collision course with this bottom, I was calling my mother frequently. I was preparing to kill myself. I so much wanted to slice my wrists. I remember sharpening the K-Bar (military knife) I had, in order to do the job quickly.

I remember one morning laying out in the yard rubbing the knife against the veins popping out of my arm. Looking at my arms, I stared at the track marks. Each one seemed to echo a thought: "Do it, and do it now." But another voice whispered, "No!" Looking back I realize it was the "still, small voice" of God's Spirit holding me back. *I* may have forgotten about accepting Christ at age eleven, but *He* hadn't. His grace is what kept me from tearing that knife vertical on my arm. During this time, my son Robbie was conceived. This added additional stress. It saddens me that to this day my son and I do not have a relationship. My hope is that God will one day put him in my life, something that I did not do.

After awhile I found myself in court, and eventually jail, because of my addiction and my violent ways. After serving three months of an eighteen-month sentence, I was released to in-house incarceration. During this time I had a series of conversations with my mother regarding going to church. She said I needed to get right with the Lord. Eventually I would take her advice. But that was a direction Stacy found herself unable to go. Choosing to follow God would lose me my girlfriend and children, but it would save my life!

But before that, I had to hit bottom. At the end, I had a large habit, which consisted of anything that would take the pain away, ranging from drugs and drinking to eating and sex. I was twenty-eight when I hit bottom. I weighed 370 pounds and was out of my mind. Most of the people I knew did not want to hang out or have anything to do with me. I was mean, unpredictable, and psychotic. Even the lowliest bars I attended no longer wanted me there. In spite of all this, I lived with an illusion that I was in control!

For most of my life up till this time, I lived with this illusion of control. I used everything possible (drugs, lying, manipulation, and intimidation) to maintain this illusion. I used it to control people around me and suppress my feelings of being lost. But light was about to dawn on this illusion and show me it was actually a big lie from Satan.

4

Being Saved

Again Jesus spoke to them, saying, "I am the light of
the world; whoever follows me will not walk in the
darkness, but will have the light of life"... So Jesus
said to the Jews who had believed him, "If you abide
in my word, you are truly my disciples, and you will
know the truth, and the truth will set you free."

—John 8:12, 31–32

The Hero and Savior

MY WHOLE LIFE up to age twenty-eight I had searched for a
hero or savior. My search brought me to drugs, people, places,
and things, but I did not find a hero and was not saved. On

the contrary, I found only disappointment and slavery. Finally I found myself searching somewhere outside of this world. There had always been a quiet voice directing me to this Person and place. The Person was Jesus, and the place was His crucifixion on the cross two thousand years before I was born.

Remembering the teaching about Jesus at my boyhood church, the Holy Spirit started to direct my path. The year was 1988. It was on a Wednesday. I went back to First Presbyterian Church in Quincy. The church had a side door that connected to the pastor's and associate pastor's offices. This is where I met the Reverend Jeff Arnold, the associate pastor for youth and discipleship.

Jeff was a small, quiet, godly, and loving man—the opposite of me! He had a special Presence he emanated. I now know it was the Holy Spirit. Jeff was just leaving for lunch and asked me if I could return the following day, which I obliged him. Later he told me he did that to test whether I was really serious about a spiritual quest. He asked me to come a little before noon. This was the place and the moment that I began the journey from brokenness into oneness.

When I arrived on Thursday, Jeff invited me into his office. He asked me if I knew Jesus. I said yes. He asked me if I had accepted him, and if I hadn't, did I want to. Within minutes I was on my knees repeating a prayer accepting Jesus in my life, once again. An indescribable feeling of both sorrow and freedom overcame me. I started crying and began asking for forgiveness, forgiveness for all the evil and harm I had caused people and myself. I gave Jeff a hug, like a grizzly bear hugging a lamb! He later admitted he was a bit intimidated at the time.

For the rest of the afternoon I was floored, humbled and broken before the Lord's oneness. It's a moment in my life I will never forget, a moment when my heart began to be changed, a moment when a new life began. The phrase has been overused today, but truly I was born again. I found my hero, Jesus; I found my Savior, Jesus; I found my Father, through Jesus; and I found a new family, because of Jesus. OORAH, now life was going to be easy… Wrong! Now that I was brought into the light of truth, life would be a journey in seasons that were both good and bad. But it would be a journey guided by One who loved me and who really *was* in control.

God's Boot Camp—The Beginning

After accepting the Lord, I now had to sober up. This would take time, and a few more bottoms. After floundering around, still getting high, I conceded my need to follow God's command about this problem. I spoke with Jeff about it, and he did some research to find me a place to start my recovery. He found a few places, but they didn't work out. As Jeff came to realize, I was just too unpredictable and volatile. I had major anger issues and destructive tendencies, and without the drugs, I didn't know how to cope. So we decided to get me into detox. I enrolled in Faxon Detox in Quincy City Hospital, where I would spend about two months in early 1989. I had to stay for such an extended period of time because halfway houses for post detox would not accept me! However, God's timing was precise, and He chose a special place for me to go and a special man to be my teacher. The special place was Hamilton House in Dorchester, Massachusetts, and the special man was Dr. Bob Brown. The House was in the middle of a drug war zone. Dr. Bob was a large gentleman who had found the Lord in his own journey. He was big and loud, like me, but also very caring. He was the one God would use to break me more, on my way to oneness. This started on my first day of four years living at the house in 1989.

That first day at the house I was scared and confused, as well as suicidal. During the days, Dr. Bob had a regimen of classes and AA or NA meetings clients had to attend. He took a special interest in me, and eventually I took a special interest in him, seeing him as a father figure. Dr. Bob and I went tooth and nail in confrontations between us during my stay at the house. God bless this man for his forbearance with me! I was a madman and would not stand down when confronted. This went on till the day I left. And I can say I was the same way with God. God was correcting the sins and habits of my past, and I have rebelled against Him in many ways, even to this day. But no matter how much I rebel, God wins, and wins, and wins. He wins by loving me unconditionally.

As time went on, I began to recover. Little did I know I had a lifetime of this ahead of me. My recovery was challenged in a major way after my first year. Since I was at risk for many diseases, from sharing needles and sleeping with many women, Bob had me go to Project Trust at Boston City Hospital to be tested. Two weeks after being tested, my whole life was turned upside down, again. It was the spring of 1991 when I was diagnosed with HIV. I was given only a few years to live. The disease was still in its infant stages of being tested, and no known antiviral medication was effective. After being diagnosed, a very close girl friend of mine died. I was devastated, and with this I wanted to die. But dying was not in God's plan.

A month or so after I was diagnosed, Dr. Bob called me into his office. He was very learned regarding Scripture and had a strong relationship with Jesus. In this relationship the Holy Spirit directed him to quote a Scripture verse to me. In his office this one day, he asked me to pray and remember a Scripture verse. We prayed for God's will, and then he gave me the verse, Proverbs 3:5–8 (see below).

> Trust in the Lord with all your heart, and do not lean on your own understanding. In all your ways acknowledge him, and he will make straight your paths. Be not wise in your own eyes; Fear the Lord, and turn away from evil. It will be healing to your flesh and refreshment to your bones. (Prov. 3:5–8)

This verse has been burned into my heart, and to this day I have used it many times in my battles against Satan. Miraculously, I have been protected not only from death, but from *any* health problems from HIV, 1991 to 2016—twenty-five years! And that has been with *no* treatment or antiviral drugs! Sometimes God does not take away or heal. Sometimes He allows things to happen or continue in our lives because there is something more important we need to learn from it. He may not change the situation but instead use the situation to change our perspective. In my life He used HIV as a tool to break me all the more and then mold my heart. This brokenness brought me one step closer to God's will for me. After my diagnosis, I made a promise not to sleep with or have intimate relationships with women. This in turn taught me how to see women in a godly, healthy way, and not as objects for my own control and gratification. I strictly kept my promise of celibacy for ten years, and then again later to the present—but more on that in chapter 18.

A few weeks after Dr. Bob gave me the verse from Proverbs, I had an experience that would have a profound impact on the rest of my life. I was living on the third floor of Hamilton House. One night I was reading the Bible when suddenly a strange sense of peace overwhelmed me. Words fail to describe it, but it was powerful and awesome! I called Bob and asked him what it was. He told me it was the Holy Spirit. On three consecutive evenings, at the same time, the

Holy Spirit met with me and anointed me. I prayed, cried, read the Bible, and contemplated God. On the final night the Holy Spirit was so overwhelming that I found myself led down to the basement where I laid face down on the floor crying. It was as if Christ was present, and there was no place low enough for me to prostrate myself in order to honor Him. My mind, heart, and soul were filled with His presence. I felt perplexed. Then I started to pray and speak in tongues. I felt led to pray this prayer: "God, squeeze all the sin out of me." Little did I realize what I was asking! It is still being answered to this day.

Remaining healthy, while watching my friends die of AIDS, diseased and struggling, I was left confused and feeling unconnected, but God's mighty hand was still upon my heart. Nevertheless, feelings of confusion and being disconnected remained a theme throughout my life. I often had feelings that God was not here for me, but this was far from the truth. Instead, Satan was using my past experiences to twist my thinking and feelings. I was soon diagnosed with two other serious diseases, syphilis and hepatitis C. Wow! One might ask, "How did you handle that?" The answer is, I didn't—*Jesus* did! With all this compounded, I also had to deal with major depression, which I still struggle with to some degree. Eventually I was diagnosed with bipolar disorder. This was and is my toughest battle. The bipolar cycle starts with a mild mania period of increased energy and feeling able to do anything. This increases to racing thoughts, grandiose plans, and dulled inhibitions—the most dangerous stage, when reckless or self-destructive behavior is likely. After this peaks, I crash into depression. My depressions started early in my recovery. They consisted of a sense of impending doom, thoughts of suicide, and feelings of paranoia. In the beginning they lasted for days and then went away. After time the cycles became shorter. Prayer, reading the Bible, and listening to radio preachers helped. But facing this onslaught of negative health conditions had further implications, which affected my dreams and aspirations, past and present. (For more about bipolar disorder, see chapter 19.)

What I did not realize at the time was that these dreams and aspirations were fueled by my having been hurt. I wanted to be wanted. With my newborn faith, I was like a little kid with new toys. I had never really dealt with my abandonment issues, and even then I did not really deal with them. I continued to maintain my illusion of being in control, but now with a newly supplied arsenal, an arsenal that I *thought* was not as destructive. On the contrary! The destruction just took a different form.

5

Growing Pains

The Illusion of Control

As I MENTIONED before, most of my life I adapted to the ways of an illusion in order to control what I was feeling and my surroundings. This illusion bound me tightly and convinced me that I was in control, when I really was not. I've mentioned my addictions and obvious sins. But it was more *deeply rooted* sins that caused me to have this illusion. Having doubts about myself, I dug deep into my arsenal of ways to control my surroundings in my new walk as a born-again believer in Jesus Christ.

This arsenal contained a mixed bag of emotions and actions from both my past and my new life. Some were obviously selfish acts like lying, which was a product of my fear, anger, frustration, hate, and envy. Others were acts that involved doing things that seemed good on the surface, a product of love, compassion, empathy, and so on. This second type of act *seemed* good but always had another, more selfish motive.

In my feelings of fear, anger, frustration, hate, and envy, I would cause others to feel the same way through intimidation, manipulation, lying, or coercion, to control them. I used my actions to transfer these feelings to them. But I did the same thing with love, compassion, and empathy! At the end of each action, whether bad or good, I was filled with myself and the vileness that comes with that. I then ran to new addictions to suppress the emptiness that came from my previous actions, and the cycle was repeated. To some degree, I am still being broken from them.

My Empire

The year was 1991 and I was living at the recovery house. Dr. Brown brought to my attention the then-current perspective regarding HIV/AIDS. The perspective was that people with HIV/AIDS were dying, and there were no funds available to help maintain the condition of someone having AIDS. He said it would be to my advantage to start a business, an electrical business. His idea was good, because he thought that I would eventually get sick. When this happened, I would need to have time and money to be treated, which the business would provide. Little did he know that God did not give me a death sentence! Little did *I* know this business would become a new addiction and tool! As it grew, it would consume me, becoming an empire that I could build at my convenience, and then add to it the things that would fulfill my illusion of control.

Using my experience as journeyman electrician, I began pounding the pavement to look for customers. The first work I got turned out not to be all electrical but involved apartment renovations, adding to my building skills—framing, tiling, plumbing, masonry, finish carpentry, and more. I worked hard, with good results, and began to get more business. I studied for and passed my masters electrical exam, and was certified to do work for the City of Boston, the state of Massachusetts, and the Federal Government. With my Chinese ethnicity, I also applied for and was certified by SOWMBA (State Office of Women and Minority Business Administration), which led to additional clients.

As I built the business, I eventually was able to hire people to work for me and benefit from their labor. This gave me time for myself. However, there were also more deep-rooted things that I needed the business/empire for. These included pride, feelings of recognition, success, and self-accomplishment, but most of all the illusion of control. The one thing I thought would gain me the control I felt

I needed was controlling me! It would take the great hand of God to break this, and He did it by literally breaking me. This would happen in 2004. There's a Scripture verse that puts my experience in perspective, Genesis 32:24–25 (see below).

> And Jacob was left alone. And a man wrestled with him until the breaking of the day. When the man saw that he did not prevail against Jacob, he touched his hip socket, and Jacob's hip was put out of joint as he wrestled with him. (Gen. 32:24–25)

Anyone who has read the story of Jacob realizes he was a manipulator. This is something I would eventually see in myself after the collapse of my business/empire. Just as Jacob wrestled with God (manifest in an angel), I also did. And God blessed me by breaking me, just as he did Jacob (even using a pelvis/hip injury!) and taking away the illusion that I was in control through my business or empire. I write more about that later.

We live in a world where people do the same thing as Jacob did and I did. This includes people from all parts of society—no one is exempt. Only by living in the Holy Spirit can people see these actions in themselves and in others. What a vexing situation we live in. It is no wonder the world has such a multitude of problems. However, there is a way to be freed. It's not a freedom that comes instantly, but a freedom that comes from a series of encounters with

Jesus. These transform and heal our brokenness, which brings oneness with God. Let me share more about how the brokenness in my life combated my illusion of control and brought the beginning of freedom.

Freedom

Truth from Jesus in my new birth showed me *His* truth, not mine, bringing freedom. Although I had His truth, there were still deep-rooted lies from my past causing destructive patterns in my life, such as justification and denial. These needed to be addressed by God's burning light. Although free from eternal death, there were still areas of sin I needed to be freed from. God's truth burned in my heart, bringing to the surface these deeper sins. This difficult and challenging process has continued throughout my Christian walk, bringing ever increasing freedom from these sins.

Working at a foundry when I was a teenager, I remember a process that was similar to this. The job I had was to prepare for the pour of a molten metal. I learned that the harder the metal, the hotter the temperature had to be. Metal being heated to a high temperature brings to the surface impurities (slag), which I would then take a ladle and scoop out. This is an example of how God's fire frees us from our deeper sins.

Being a hard metal, or hardheaded, the fire of God's truth had to be pretty hot to bring to the surface my impurities (i.e. sins). As I brought them to the cross, Jesus would scoop them away with His gentle hand, bringing freedom. This is similar to Paul's description in 2 Corinthians 4 of God's truth and power working through his trials to produce a life that is freer from sin (see Scripture below).

> But we have this treasure in jars of clay, to show that the surpassing power belongs to God and not to us. We are afflicted in every way, but not crushed; perplexed, but not driven to despair; persecuted, but not forsaken; struck down, but not destroyed; always carrying in the body the death of Jesus, so that the life of Jesus may also be manifested in our bodies. For we who live are always being given over to death for Jesus' sake, so that the life of Jesus also may be manifested in our mortal flesh. So death is at work in us, but life in you. (2 Cor. 4:7–12)

Dreams

From a young age, we learn that having a good education, job, spouse, and family is the goal we should try to attain. The Cinderella story, a nice home surrounded by a white picket fence, children playing in the yard, becomes the dream. Coming from a dysfunctional home, I all the more wanted this dream. When I accepted Christ, I thought, "Now that I am a Christian, these will come true." Even truer, in fact, than the fairy tale, since they would follow God's design.

I dreamed of having a godly relationship with a woman, practicing purity as I waited for marriage, and having a relationship based on love rather than lust and sex. But this would not happen, and to this day, it still has not. When one grows in Christ, one's dreams and aspirations change, and eventually I would learn the truth that God knows what is best for me. A relationship with a woman was not in God's will for me, and to this day I think this is still true. But I sometimes wish God would give these things to me.

In spite of my new birth in Christ, many of the actual dreams I experienced at night were nightmares. Nightmares that rose from the grave of my past, nightmares of shooting dope in a shooting gallery, nightmares of violence and wickedness, causing me to have sleep problems and feelings of paranoia. Many times I said to myself, "Oh God, why? Why don't you take them away?" Eventually I learned this was one more way God was refining and teaching me. God used these as a tool to help me stay dependent on Him. In the back of my nightmares lurked a dark figure accusing and tempting me with my sins. It would be safe to say it was Satan. God was warning me about my adversary.

At the same time, there were also new dreams, dreams of hope for people, people accepting Christ in large numbers, children embracing Christ, people gathered in worship, and me being with Jesus worshipping God. When I had these latter dreams, I would wake up with a refreshing new energy that could only come from the Holy Spirit.

I still have these types of scenes in my nightmares and dreams; however, it seems as if the nightmares are often more vivid. I believe this is because of the clarity God is giving me regarding spiritual battles, helping me see that I have an adversary, whose overall purpose is to take me down. (For more about this spiritual warfare, see chapter 25.) Life is not going to be a day at the beach just because I became a Christian. But it does have its moments!

One of those moments happened in my early days as a Christian, when God blessed me with a new dream and a gift. One day Pastor Jeff and I were hanging around the church. Going outside to the back, Jeff showed me where a couple of windows were damaged. In the parking lot were some boys playing basketball. Jeff asked if they broke the windows, but they did not respond. With my characteristic loudness, I followed up by asking them, "Who broke these windows?"

Slightly intimidated, they replied, "We didn't. Someone else did!"

After this I was able to strike up a conversation with them. Jeff was taken by this and said to me, "Eric, here is your ministry—youth!" Little did we know the Holy Spirit planted this comment as well as blessing me with a gift to connect with troubled youth. From that day forward, God has blessed me with many volunteer opportunities to work with young people, and many of them have come to Christ and grown in Him. This thread of youth ministry is a theme that has run throughout my life since that moment.

Youth Ministry

Attending church and actively volunteering to work with youth throughout the years, God has used me to present the gospel, plant seeds, and lead many youth away from the destructive life they were choosing, into a relationship with Jesus Christ. The youth came from the full spectrum of society: from small-town country kids to suburban church kids to urban street kids, from the well-to-do spiritual skeptic to the homeless valedictorian who loved Jesus and had a different color hair every time I saw her, from every type of social or religious background, a patchwork quilt of colorful young lives woven together in my life by the thread of youth ministry.

At the beginning of this ministry, God put a strange character in my life, a character who had many abilities, especially in English. This man is Charlie Winkelman, the one going through the painful, daunting, and vexing process of editing this book! Charlie was hired as the associate pastor for youth and discipleship at First Presbyterian Church in Quincy in 1991, the successor to my friend Pastor Jeff Arnold when he moved on to become the founding pastor of a new church. I volunteered to help Charlie lead the youth group at the church.

Charlie and I work well together, and we have been working with youth for over twenty-four years. We have worked together creating and leading youth programs such as service projects, social events, weekend retreats, summer mission trips, and weekly youth group fellowship meetings with games, Bible study, discussion, and snacks. Charlie has a fun-loving mischievous side and could get me to do anything in the beginning; however, I have learned many of his tactics! Let me share a story.

We were preparing a talent show competition for the youth group. Youth from other churches were invited as well. The kids had many talents, such as singing, acting, and playing musical instruments. The only talent I had was being big and loud. So Charlie, in his great love for me, decided to help me with this problem! He told me I could act! I was really excited! Acting—OORAH, Marine Corps, I thought. Maybe I will be famous, I thought to myself. I had never acted in anything before! Getting ready for the day of the show, my anticipation and enthusiasm were increasing. Everyone was practicing, making their costumes, and getting ready. For me, my costume was my skin, meaning my chest and belly. Charlie's activity for me was to paint a face on my front side using my chest as eyes, my arms as ears and my belly button as the mouth. I was excited, thinking the kids would get a big kick out of this.

The call to the stage came. I was the very first act! With great excitement and a front side painted as a face, I stood behind the curtain with anticipation for some fun. I could hear Charlie announcing the greatest act to ever open a talent show, an alien from another planet! That was me! The curtain rose to the dramatic opening trumpet fanfare of the film *2001 A Space Odyssey*. As the tympani pounded in the music, I started to wiggle my chest, shake my arms, and bounce around my belly moving the lips. But surprise! Sitting in front of me were not just the kids, as I had expected, but all the *parents* as well! Somehow in all the pre-show hype, Charlie had forgotten to mention this little detail! Professionals, school teachers, and business people—all watching me bounce my flubber around to a trumpet fanfare! The room exploded in hilarious laughter! I ended and humbly jiggled off the stage after the music stopped, to great applause. All the youth had fun and did a great job in the acts that followed. When it came time to hand out the awards, mine was presented first. I received the award for being a good sport. I will never forget this experience, especially since the youth (and parents) kept talking about it for years!

Youth ministry can be great fun, and this is one time that was both awesome and humbling. On the other hand, there are the areas in youth ministry that teach the great, life-changing truths of the Gospel. The talent show and other fun events helped build relationships. With relationships, the youth learned they could trust us and bring us into their culture. Eventually they would share their concerns about life. Many committed their lives to Christ for the first time and grew in their faith and walk with Him.

There are many of the youth I hold dearly in my heart. I mentioned Matt Fuccillo in the first chapter. Let me note two others. I received a letter in 1998; it appears I had a big influence on a young man named Michael Bober. He was tall and quiet. He was touched by the fact that an ex-drug addict and tough person like me could find Christ. In this letter he stated how he had accepted the Lord because of our relationship. He went on to say how accepting Christ changed his life.

Another story concerns a heavyset young man who had an odor problem. He was led to learn more about Christ because I was able to challenge him regarding the smell and how he presented himself. He was a loner and stood outside in the back before church. Christ calling me, I stepped out and took him into my life. After doing this, it was like night and day. After I left, the new youth minister, David Rockness, was able to continue the ministry with the young man, enabling him to admit and repent of activities on the Internet that were not conducive to his growth.

Later I moved down to Virginia to be closer to my family, where I volunteered and became youth leader at the Springhill Presbyterian Church, leading young people in many of the same activities we had done in Quincy, as well as interacting with them on an individual basis (see chapter 7). There too I was thrilled to see God changing lives as I opened my life to His working in and through me.

I could go on and on. These youth know who they are, and they now know the love of Christ, and how, because of accepting Him, they have eternal life, which changed everything about them. I am so thankful God gave me the privilege of helping them. The fact that God could redeem my terrible past as a tool to help me reach out to kids, especially at-risk kids, shows His amazing grace toward me and also these youth. I pray that my story will continue to help young people come to know and love the Lord.

Recently I have volunteered at Big Brothers and Big Sisters. This is a great ministry that has produced awesome fruit. In the last several years, I befriended a young boy named Malcolm, my "little" as defined by Big Brothers and Big Sisters. Malcolm accepted Christ, and soon his sister also accepted Christ! The seeds were planted. The whole family, all six of them, plus some cousins, have started going to church! Without the open-mindedness of the director and others at Big Brothers and Big Sisters, I would not have been able to do this. They truly have a love for kids.

Today I work with the youth groups and also a new After School Kids (ASK) program with my friend Charlie at the Jersey Shore Presbyterian Church. This program involves a weekly after-school program with kids from the neighborhood surrounding the church, with homework help, fun games or crafts, Bible teaching, prayer, snacks, and sometimes ringing the church bell! As this ministry expands, and combines with youth groups and Sunday School, we are seeing Jesus impact whole families! And I believe that Bailey, Beckah, Breeann, Savannah, Sierra, Olivia, Victoria, Elizabeth, Ella, Quinn, Val, Dilon, Bryce, Corbin, Dustin, Chiara, Malcolm, Emma, Levi, Bella, and Emily, just the latest in a long line of very special kids, will enjoy seeing their name in a book, and more importantly, in the Book of Life!

6

The Blessing and the Pearl

The Blessing and My Dad

RETURNING NOW TO my personal struggles after I accepted Christ, as I mentioned I had ill will against my parents, especially my father. As I participated in a three-man Bible study with my friends, Charlie Winkelman and Steve Emery, they tuned in to this. I had told my mother on many occasions that if my father should die, I would spit on his grave. One day I admitted to Charlie and Steve that I wanted to kill him. Deep inside me boiled a rage because of all the abuse, and him not being there for me, made worse by the attention he was giving to his new wife's children. I blamed him for the life of hell I had been through. Deep down in my soul, I knew this murderous rage was wrong. But I just could not forgive my dad for all he had done.

Seeing my rage, Charlie suggested that I read a book called *The Blessing*, by John Trent and Gary Smalley. So I did, and WOW! Did God ever use this book to show me His will! My whole life I had looked for my parents and especially my father to bless me. This book showed me how my father's lack of blessing me stemmed from *him* never having received the blessing from *his* father. Using this book, the Holy Spirit led me to believe I had to forgive my father and bless him. I will tell you that this did not sit well with me. But I saw that because of what Jesus did for me, I needed to do the same for my father.

Looking in Scripture, one can see how powerful these blessings are, and how the *lack* of blessing can be so damaging.

> So [Jacob] came near and kissed [his father Isaac]; and Isaac smelled the smell of his garments and blessed him and said, "See, the smell of my son is as the smell of a field that the Lord has blessed! May God give you of the dew of heaven and of the fatness of the earth and plenty of grain and wine. Let peoples serve you, and nations bow down to you. Be lord over your brothers, and may your mother's sons bow down to you. Cursed be everyone who curses you, and blessed be everyone who blesses you!"

As soon as Isaac had finished blessing Jacob, when Jacob had scarcely gone out from the presence of Isaac his father, Esau his brother came in from his hunting. He also prepared delicious food and brought it to his father. And he said to his father, "Let my father arise and eat of his son's game, that you may bless me." His father Isaac said to him, "Who are you?" He answered, "I am your son, your first-born, Esau." Then Isaac trembled very violently and said, "Who was it then that hunted game and brought it to me, and I ate it all before you came, and I have blessed him? Yes, and he shall be blessed."

As soon as Esau heard the words of his father, he cried out with an exceedingly great and bitter cry and said to his father, "Bless me, even me also, O my father!" But he said, "Your brother came deceitfully, and he has taken away your blessing." (Gen. 27:27–35)

In Genesis 27, the story of Isaac's blessing for his sons, Jacob and Esau, depicts how important a blessing can be, both to the one who is being blessed and to the one who is not. Jacob was blessed by his father Isaac. Even though he *stole* his brother Esau's blessing by deceit, he was still blessed! One can see the effects on both Jacob and Esau. In the "exceedingly great and bitter cry," you can hear in Esau his anguish. But to understand the blessing, one has to see and experience what Esau did despite being cheated out of his blessing. Moving to Genesis 33, after the brothers have been apart for many years, we see Esau doing the very thing that *I* was being asked to do.

> But Esau ran to meet [Jacob] and embraced him
> and fell on his neck and kissed him, and they wept.
> (Gen. 33:4)

God had asked me to do this, to bless the one who in effect had "stolen" the blessing from me. The opportunity came to fruition. My father was going through a nasty legal battle with his second wife and had to come to Boston. I was thirty-six years old and living in Quincy at this time. It was the spring of 1994. Life was going well for me, as my business thrived and my volunteer youth work was bearing fruit. Trying to be obedient to God's will as I had seen it in *The Blessing*, I invited my father to stay with me for a week. He came, and to my delight, God was able to use those seven days so that I could bless my father, just as Esau blessed his brother. I was able do this despite the contempt I had for him. This action became the basis and onset for a new relationship with my father! I am not going to say all my anger and rage went away immediately. But I can honestly say that because I followed God's will in this matter, it brought forth a better relationship with my dad, as well as with others. This is because true blessings are not in the receiving, but in the giving. Even despite years of abandonment and abuse that I had endured, God worked a miracle of blessing and forgiveness in my heart toward my dad. Eventually my dad himself even accepted Christ!

During many of my nights listening to radio preachers, I was encouraged by what I heard regarding other blessings. Charles Stanley has said many times how his mother blessed him, how he knows her voice, and how, because of God's blessings, he was also able to bless his stepfather despite his feelings. Ravi Zacharias talked about a time when he went back to India where his grandmother was buried and received a blessing from a Scripture verse on her head stone. Chuck Swindol talks about the many blessings he gives as a result of being blessed by his parents. James Dobson talks about how his father blessed him by hunting and fishing with him when he was younger, and because of this, he has been able to bless people with a valuable ministry, "Focus on the Family." Furthermore, Dr. Dobson was able to interview Ted Bundy and give the blessing despite the contempt the public had for this born-again believer who was once a vicious serial killer. One could say that if God forgave the Apostle Paul, despite him being a murderer and persecutor of the early church, God could do the same for Ted Bundy, and for any who repent and accept God's grace and forgiveness through Jesus Christ.

I believe that there are many more people for whom blessing is waiting just around the corner. Not the blessing of material wealth, but of restored relationships with God and others. Love is best expressed when you love despite adversity, contempt, and other negative actions toward you. True love involves reaching your heart and hand out to others, even when they have hurt you, and it produces unexpected feelings of peace and contentment. Although difficult to do, oneness with God in actions of love and forgiveness brings oneness in other relationships. This can be seen in what are called the Beatitudes (which means blessings) from Jesus' Sermon on the Mount in the Gospel of Matthew and from the Apostle's John's first letter (see below).

The Beatitudes

Seeing the crowds, [Jesus] went up on the mountain, and when he sat down, his disciples came to him. And he opened his mouth and taught them, saying:

"Blessed are the poor in spirit, for theirs is the kingdom of heaven.

Blessed are those who mourn, for they shall be comforted.

Blessed are the meek, for they shall inherit the earth.

Blessed are those who hunger and thirst for righteousness, for they shall be satisfied.

Blessed are the merciful, for they shall receive mercy.

Blessed are the pure in heart, for they shall see God.

Blessed are the peacemakers, for they shall be called sons of God.

Blessed are those who are persecuted for righteousness' sake, for theirs is the kingdom of heaven.

Blessed are you when others revile you and persecute you and utter all kinds of evil against you falsely on my account. Rejoice and be glad, for your reward is great in heaven, for so they persecuted the prophets who were before you." (Matt. 5:1–12)

Many times in my life I have been called to rise above my circumstances. At these times God has often reached into my heart and reminded me of Scripture that He has put there through the Holy Spirit, my studying, and listening. For example, like everyone else, I have had to mourn many times. From the Beatitudes in Matthew, I learned "Blessed are those who mourn, for they shall be comforted." As I have mourned for others as well as myself, mourned over my own sinfulness, and mourned over the brokenness not only in my own life but in the lives of those who hurt me, God has miraculously provided both grace and opportunities for forgiveness and reconciliation that have brought the comfort of God for myself and others. Likewise, I experienced Jesus' promise "Blessed are the merciful, for they shall obtain mercy." As I have experienced God's mercy toward me in all of my failings, it has led me to have mercy on others as well, and in this I experienced God's mercy myself all the more.

> By this we know love, that [Jesus] laid down his life for us; and we ought to lay down our lives for the brothers. But if anyone has the world's goods and sees his brother in need, yet closes his heart against him, how does God's love abide in him? Little children, let us not love in word or talk but in deed and in truth. (1 John 3:16–18)

There are many more such examples, but they are all summed up in God's call to love my brother in 1 John 3. Loving my brother is really showing love for everyone, laying down my life for others in real practical deeds that demonstrate the truth of God's love for us. This genuine unconditional love that flows from God through my heart to others, that brings God's great blessing, is at the crucial center of the kingdom of God, the "pearl of great value" we would gladly surrender all to gain.

The Heart and the Pearl

The heart encapsulates many things, especially the past with all its negative emotions and sins, just like an oyster covers irritating sand particles with mother of pearl to keep them from hurting. When we accept Christ, these negative emotions and sins are covered by His blood.

Again, the kingdom of heaven is like a merchant in search of fine pearls, who, on finding one pearl of great value, went and sold all that he had and bought it. (Matt. 13:45–46)

Our heart is the same way. We must relinquish all to find the kingdom of God—the pearl of great value. Because of the way a pearl is made, it is an appropriate symbol for this:

The birth of a pearl is truly a miraculous event. Unlike gemstones or precious metals that must be mined from the earth, pearls are grown by live oysters far below the surface of the sea. Gemstones must be cut and polished to bring out their beauty. But pearls need no such treatment to reveal their loveliness. They are born from oysters complete, with a shimmering iridescence, luster and soft inner glow unlike any other gem on earth.

A natural pearl begins its life as a foreign object, such as a grain of sand or a piece of shell, that accidentally lodges itself in an oyster's soft inner body where it cannot be expelled. To ease this irritant, the oyster's body takes defensive action. The oyster begins to secrete a smooth, hard crystalline substance around the irritant in order to protect itself. This substance is called "nacre." As long as the irritant remains within its body, the oyster will continue to secrete nacre around it, layer upon layer. Over time, the irritant will be completely encased by the silky crystalline coatings. The result, ultimately, is the lovely and lustrous gem called a pearl. (Americanpearl.com)

Just as a pearl comes from a foreign object that irritates the oyster inside, its defenses protecting it using a substance called nacre, so also my past sins were hurting my heart, and God's love through His Son's death on the cross covered those sins. The result, ultimately, was a lovely and lustrous gem called a pearl—the pearl of love. In the process of making a pearl, something bad brings to fruition something good.

It was not by man's hand, such as polishing or psychoanalysis, but by an internal process of the Holy Spirit that God brought forth His pearl of love in me. As His Spirit probed my heart, it revealed my deepest intentions, which could be seen in my actions. Jesus said from out of the heart come the evil thoughts and actions that defile a man.[1] Deep in my heart were the irritants or sinful intentions of pride and selfishness. The Holy Spirit and the word of God can reveal these by bringing them to the surface of my consciousness, and cleanse my heart from them with the blood of Jesus—His death that bought my forgiveness and freedom from sin. But when this happens, deep emotional pain accompanies the surfacing. The pain brings depression and further negative feelings. Running to external comforts is then my first inclination, and sometimes this happens. God knows this and comforts me with His love as I read His word, love others, and believe

---

[1] See Matthew 15:17–20.

His promises. In this comfort I have learned His truth, that as He loves me, so I must love all.

> But thanks be to God, that you who were once slaves of sin have become obedient from the heart to the standard of teaching to which you were committed, and, having been set free from sin, have become slaves of righteousness. I am speaking in human terms, because of your natural limitations. For just as you once yielded your members to impurity and to greater and greater iniquity, so now yield your members to righteousness for sanctification. (Rom. 6:17–19, RSV)

So you can see in my experience the conflict between the word of God and the sin in my heart, like the conflict between the oyster and the foreign object in a pearl. What is hidden in my heart is deep. But God's word is "living and active, sharper than any two-edged sword, piercing to the division of soul and spirit, of joints and marrow, and discerning the thoughts and intentions of the heart."[2] His word is eternal, and from it comes eternal comfort even in the hell of negative emotions. The blessing—me blessing my father—as simple as it may seem, is just one tool that God used to make my past, although negative and irritable, into a pearl in its entire luster. I have always

---

[2]   Hebrews 4:12, RSV

been very analytical, but in all my thinking, I cannot break myself free from my past. I have found that applying the Scripture verses above from the Beatitudes has dealt with many irritants. What I am learning is that God's timing is important, and that nothing I can do can cleanse the sins from my heart aside from His intervention. The miracle is the outcome—God's love with shimmering iridescence, luster, and soft inner glow unlike anything on earth. In Christ we all have in our heart a special pearl, resulting in God's righteousness. No two pearls are exactly alike; each one is special, the heart and the pearl!

7

Weathering the Storms

Booming Business and Broken Body

Applying the word of God regarding blessing my father was just one of many events up to now. By this time I was thirty-five. Things were okay. I had a growing electrical business, New View Electrical, Inc., and God was providing work from both private and public clients. When I was building my business, I was able to be certified through the State Office of Women and Minority Business Administration (SOWMBA) certification from the division of Capital Planning of the City of Boston. This certification brought contracts from larger companies, requiring a larger crew. I decided to bring in a partner, which brought additional resources to help with the additional work.

Soon after being certified by the City of Boston, my company was awarded a contract renovating the electrical apparatus at half-round roofed skating rinks in Dedham, Massachusetts. Apparently the roofs from many caved in after a vicious snow storm ran through the area. Getting this contract was a wonderful success and a great opportunity.

Unfortunately, it was also the occasion for an injury that took me down. It was June of 1995. Reviewing the job, my partner and I decided to erect scaffolding around a corridor where conduits were attached to the wall and roof trusses. The scaffolding would enable us to secure the electrical conduits during the removal and installation of new roof trusses. While building the scaffolding (which was forty feet high), we had to pull up each section from one stage to another. It was a huge job, installing two hundred sections. While pulling up one of the sections, I incurred a massive cervical C4/C5 hernia in my neck. Even worse, it took five months and a series of specialists before the injury was accurately diagnosed. All the feeling in my right arm had started to fade. When the diagnosis was finally made, my doctor put me on high doses of pain relievers and scheduled a surgery in two weeks. He told me if I had gone much longer I would have lost much of my ability to use my arm. To this day I have a high level of chronic pain from this injury.

Surgery and the Storm After

After surgery I had to recover. This was no small task. Recovery from surgery, for an ex-junkie, means getting off of the pain killers. Having been sent home after one week of recovery at the hospital, I found myself alone and worrying. I was single with no family to help care for me. The church chipped in, but I needed more extensive ongoing care. When I called my insurance company, they informed they were not going to pay for a visiting nurse, or even medical bills and workman's compensation. That evening, compounded with this news, I had a temperature of 105. My neighbor dropped in to see how I was. His intentions were friendly, but he came that evening with a bag of dope. In a scattered downward mental moment, I found myself with a needle in my arm again, after six years of sobriety. I was extremely out of my mind for the next couple days. I made the decision to go into detox again. After being there for a day, my arm started to swell. It seems I had gotten an aggressive bacteria from one of the needles I used. My arm was as big as my leg. Detox sent me to Boston City hospital. There they drained the poison out of my arm and helped me gather my thoughts. After being released, I still had no one to take care of me. So I decided to move down to Virginia where my family now lived. It was now August of 1995.

Moving to Virginia brought about a great deal of personal loss. Loss of income, loss of a successful business

I built from scratch, loss of church and friends, but especially the loss of me. I was confused, I was angry, and most of all, again, I felt abandoned by people. I sold my company to my partner, and he destroyed it. I moved down to Staunton, Virginia, where my mother, father (separate from my mother), sister, and brother now lived. In physical pain and reeling emotionally from the move and sense of loss, I began my recovery lying on a single bed in a room of the storage building where my mother worked, the only quarters available on short notice. Disappointingly, I received very little support from my family. I asked myself why—why didn't my parents want to help, why did God let this all happen, and why did I feel that no matter what I did, I was a failure? Deep in my heart I could not feel God's love for me. What I felt was how I was a dummy and a failure and therefore *could* not feel and know God's love. These feelings, and rising above them, would become a big part of my continuing journey.

From a very young age, around twelve, I had to get up each morning and work long hours, go days without eating, endure abuse of all kinds, drive myself, and move forward. I had learned to rise above. I did this well, and in many cases by my own will. As I grew in my knowledge of God's word, I learned that in many cases my doing this was opposite of God's will. I became dependent upon myself, leaving no room for God. But God continued to address this in my life. I needed to be broken more, in order to become one with

God and His plan for me. At the time I did not see that the one thing I built was the one thing that would take me down—pride. Because I was searching for externalities to cover up my painful experiences, I used my business and work to do the same things that drugs, alcohol, sex, and money had done for me earlier. With a business, I could control my heart, and what was encapsulated so deep within. I could keep my past at bay by using the stature of owning a business and my pride in my work! But what we gain in *this* world on our own is nothing compared to the greatness that comes from really and truly knowing and doing God's will! His will is tireless; His love penetrates every fiber of our being. This is a small but very poignant lesson I had to be broken to learn. So I received again my life from God's grace, leaving the things of the world to the world. This lesson I would have to go through one more time, but more on that later.

> For no one can lay a foundation other than that which is laid, which is Jesus Christ. Now if anyone builds on the foundation with gold, silver, precious stones, wood, hay, straw – each one's work will become manifest; for the Day will disclose it, because it will be revealed by fire, and the fire will test what sort of work each one has done. If the work that anyone has built on the foundation survives, he will receive a reward. If anyone's work is burned up, he will suffer loss, though he himself will be saved, but only as through fire. (1 Cor. 3:11–15)

Rising above this storm, I pulled myself up by my boot straps, prayed to God asking for His will, only to proceed to build another empire: "my will"—an empire of my own making. This empire I could use as before, both to hide and to control my emotions. The new empire consisted of multiple businesses. I re-created New View Electrical and slowly built the foundation and infrastructure. As the years went by, I added two other companies. One was a plumbing company, and the other was a building construction company. Business as planned went very well. I went from doing $60,000 a year in receipts to $400,000. My empire became very lucrative! I had a fat paycheck, financial freedom, and a boatload of benefits. The one thing I did not realize was that these benefits were of the world, and these businesses were not God's intention for me. This whole empire would eventually come tumbling down. The dates of these endeavors were 1996 to 2004. The description of their downfall must wait till later in my story.

Directing Youth at Springhill Presbyterian Church

Living in Virginia, I started attending Springhill Presbyterian Church, a small country church where my mother was a member. I again volunteered to work with the young people, as I had in Quincy, and was surprised to be offered the role of volunteer youth director of their small youth group, which I accepted! Once again God gave me the privilege of using his awesome gift of working with kids, seeing them come to Christ or have a seed of His truth planted in their hearts. At this church also He extended His grace by the Holy Spirit working through my actions.

The church members were country folk, with quiet ways, but they were about to see and experience something quite new to them! When I was volunteering at First Presbyterian Church in Quincy, I had been given the name "Big and Loud." I was never one to be quiet. I was frank in my opinion and was not scared to move against social norms. Springhill Presbyterian wasn't sure what to make of this large, loud, tattooed Chinese-American who spoke truth as he saw it! The youth were awesome. They saw my ways to be different but inviting. We did Bible lessons and had fun activities.

My friend, Charlie Winkelman, had been called to be the youth pastor of a church in Indiana a few years before my move to Virginia. In 1999 Charlie invited me to come speak at a community-wide World Vision 30-Hour Famine co-sponsored by his youth group. It was one of the largest 30-Hour Famine lock-ins ever held in America! Many of the 367 youth at the Famine responded to my testimony and the following altar call invitation, either accepting Christ for the first time or coming forward for prayer about other issues. God was using me and even the story of my past to reach out to kids who were also experiencing brokenness and yearning for oneness.

As I said earlier, Springhill was a small town, and the birthplace of my mother and her siblings. My mother once told me a delightful story. When she was young and attending this church, she had to walk five miles from the farm. She had one pair of church shoes. These shoes would not be put on until she arrived at church, after walking five miles *barefoot* on the dirt roads through the most beautiful valley, alongside the Middle River where her family history was centered. When my mother told me this story, a tear ran down her cheek as she thought about how things had changed. Today the roads are asphalt, but the history of her family and childhood is still there.

Regarding the children of the church, most came from brokenness, but they found enjoyment and escape running barefoot in the grass, wading in the rivers, and enjoying to some degree the innocence of youth. Nevertheless, their hearts also encapsulated the abuse and suffering they had endured.

My sister Donna was my assistant youth leader, and she connected well with the children. They accepted her and me into their culture, and we developed a level of trust. With this we learned things I choose not to talk about. Abuse and neglect can be found anywhere, no matter what level of social strata or cultural environment. Through a season we connected and built relationships. And for other seasons, the children grew to know God and accept Jesus. Swimming and hanging down by the river with them, I would regress into my past remembering the good times in Springhill, bringing out the child in me. This activity was a great time and something the kids enjoyed. We spent weekends and hours swimming, talking, and sharing our emotions at the river. This was a special place and time God made for the little ones. It was also an escape from the dreaded home living some were exposed to. But God was making some more pearls.

The Storm of Failing in Marriage

My new businesses were doing well. The companies had been awarded contracts to renovate houses, build additions, wire factories, and do other electrical and plumbing work. My partners seemed competent and honest from my perspective, although this would not be the case later as income increased. Soon they became greedy and started to dip dishonestly by entering wrong information on time cards, and also buying supplies on the company dime for their moonlighting, something I would not discover until much later. I was working long hours, as well as maintaining a growing youth group and also leading an older women's Bible study at church.

But then something happened to take me away from my responsibilities. I met a woman on the Internet, whom I would eventually marry! (For the in-depth story of this relationship, see chapter 18.) I had joined a dating website for people who have HIV. I received an e-mail one evening regarding a Christian woman who wanted to meet me. She lived in Australia and also had HIV. She explained how she was a Christian and was planning to come to the States. I made arrangements for her to stay with a Christian family I knew during her visit. It was February of 2000. I was excited and had high expectations. I thought that God was perhaps going to answer my prayer and give me the fairy-tale romance and marriage I had dreamed about! Little did I know this would be the beginning of one of the biggest storms of my life. During her thirty-day visit, I found myself choosing to break my vow to God of celibacy before marriage. It was a decision I have been paying for even to this day. Little did I know at that time that she was not actually a true Christian, by her own later admission. The devil can come in different forms and use our thoughts and dreams to deceive us.

Losing my celibacy, I came to know the type of romantic feelings that come from sleeping and having sex with a woman you really care about, something I never felt before because of my drug abuse. As many women as I had slept with, I never felt such overwhelming feelings as these. Having broken my vow to God, I found myself "in lust" with this woman. My infatuation would take me away from my business as I chased my lust to China, Hong Kong, Australia, and Hawaii, completely depleting my savings over the course of three years. With intentional sin in my life, my focus became self-centered, and I was blinded to the immorality of my actions. It seems as if Satan was always at the door waiting with a new weapon to destroy and take me down.

In spite of my sin, God in His grace redeemed some of this time for His purposes by letting me work at an orphanage in China, and smuggle Bibles and Christian literature to the underground church there. Besides the wisdom from God that comes though failure, this was the only real good that came from this relationship. In February of 2002 we got married, which was not well-received by my family in Virginia. Shortly afterward, her father died in China. She had to go back to comfort her mother and help move her family to Australia. I went along for support. When I left China, my wife stayed to support her family. She would never return.

The Storm of Failing in Business

Sitting in my office on October 25, 2002, the evening of my birthday, I was feeling sorry for myself. My wife did not want to come back. I had just fired a partner of my plumbing company for purchasing material on my account and exploiting one of my customers. I had uncovered some misbehavior by my building company partner that occurred while I was trotting around the globe. His antics resulted in court cases that combined to tie up a great deal of money. I had unwisely bankrolled all three companies with my personal finances, which were now being challenged. It became apparent that my partner was not just failing to fulfill his role, but was also skimming money off the top! I eventually fired him, which left me with many court cases, a load of debt, and a huge amount of work to accomplish shorthanded. I was overwhelmed and slowly slid into the depths of despair, losing my mind. It was December of 2002 when I slipped back into the pit of drug addiction.

Even though I was getting high, I decided to venture into an endeavor I thought would help stabilize my finances. The plan was to finance, build, and sell an expensive house in an upper class neighborhood, using the proceeds to bail out my business debts. I signed my name over and began to build the house. But my plan for financial stability was doomed. Out of my mind, with creditors calling, and losing control of my addiction, I found myself running off to Texas, leaving the business in the care of my sister. I had a cousin who was a missionary to Mexico. I thought if I spent time helping the poor in Mexico it would help. Unfortunately, it did not. External physical efforts, no matter how worthy, could not solve what was really an internal spiritual problem. After spending three months in and out of Mexico helping the poor, I found myself driving back to Virginia to try to put the pieces back together.

The Storm of Failing Health

Still chained to my addictions, I worked on my house and was able to get it framed and under roof. But what followed next was the end, as God allowed an incident that would finally break through my illusion of control and self-sufficiency. As I was standing in front of my office one day talking to a new hire, a freak accident occurred. One of my workers hopped in one of my trucks parked there, started it, and popped the clutch without realizing it was in first gear rather than reverse. The truck leapt forward, crushing me against the wall. By some miracle I was able to push the truck away from me, but then I slowly fell to the ground. I was in shock and could barely move. My sister called the ambulance, and I was rushed off to the hospital. X-rays showed my pelvis was completely broken in half, with a three-fourths-inch canal running from top to bottom. The doctor quickly sent me to the University of Virginia to undergo emergency surgery. His concern was the possibility of a severed artery, which they did not see, but which happens in nine out of ten cases of this nature. By God's grace I was one of the tenth cases. My doctor later said that God was with me. If the artery had been severed, my chances of living would have been very slim.

The trip to UVA was painful although they had administered high doses of morphine. The morphine only helped me maintain. Upon arriving, they immediately sent me to the emergency ward. They took a boatload of X-rays to find out what surgery and procedures were needed. Within twenty-four hours they had me under the knife. They installed one pin, which would prove ineffective in stabilizing the problem. I went home to recover lying on a hospital bed in my office, in extreme pain. After a few weeks, a follow-up examination showed that there were problems, and my doctors scheduled a second surgery. This time they peeled me open to get to the pelvis. When the surgery was done, they had added two additional pins and two plates. From my neck down to my ankle, I was black-and-blue. After the surgery I had to remain in the hospital at the University of Virginia for two weeks. I had lost a great deal of blood and acquired a high fever, raising concerns of infection. Having HIV and hepatitis C brought additional possible complications. After the fever was under control and I was stable, I was sent back to my hospital bed in my office.

Coming home was not easy. I had little support and was battling addiction. While recovering, I tried to maintain a drowning business and also take care of myself. My family held me in contempt, as they had when I was younger! I had to do many things on my own, with very little help. I do not want to go into great detail because I would be playing the blame game, and in the end, I was my own worst enemy. What I do know is that not many understood. It is safe to say that I was again out of my mind. In one year's time I had lost my wife, lost my financial freedom, lost my new home, lost a successful business, incurred a ton of debt, lost my ability to work, lost most of my ability to walk from being crushed by a truck, almost lost my life, and found myself running to drugs to cope.

Count it all joy, my brothers, when you meet trials of various kinds, for you know that the testing of your faith produces steadfastness. And let steadfastness have its full effect, that you may be perfect and complete, lacking in nothing…

Blessed is the man who remains steadfast under trial, for when he has stood the test he will receive the crown of life, which God has promised to those who love him. Let no one say when he is tempted, "I am being tempted by God," for God cannot be tempted with evil, and he himself tempts no one. (James 1:2–4, 12–13)

Broken and at the end of my rope, I called my friend, Charlie Winkelman, now pastoring a church in Jersey Shore, Pennsylvania, for help. He came through at my time of great need. He and his wife made a decision to take me in so I could recover. I also decided to go into a thirty-day program at the VA hospital to get off all the pain killers and drugs.

After committing myself to the VA, I was moved to the psych ward for a period of time. They reconfirmed the diagnosis of bipolar disorder. Deep in my mind and heart I tried to maintain my faith that God would help me, and He did. Not in the way I wanted it, the quick fix, a million dollar lottery ticket, but in a different way, teaching me to be still and know that He is God, to be patient and depend on Him. He knew my future, that I still had to undergo additional surgeries, two total hip replacements and a rotator cuff surgery.

Most of my life I had been able to pull myself up by my boot straps and rise above any situation. I was taught from a very young age to depend on myself, because no one else would be there for me. This was deep rooted. I had no faith in people, because when I did, they failed and failed miserably. This came from my childhood when I looked for support from my parents and others, only to be disappointed.

The Storm of Selfish "Faith"

This brings me to the subject of faith. I thought I had faith. But I learned from God during this storm that I had a "faith with strings," or *convenient* faith. True faith does not come from me, it comes from God. It is not something for my convenience, to get what I want. Faith is often rather *in*convenient, because it is about trusting God for what *He* wants. God in His love saved me. God is a God of love, who does what is best for me. This is not always what I *want*, but what I *need*. Faith is best expressed when someone acts in love even when weighed down physically, mentally, and emotionally by the storms of life.

I had a degree of faith, but it was tainted. It was a choosing faith, meaning if God gave me choices based on His will, I would add my own and think that my will was really His. I put God in a box. I thought faith meant trusting that God would give me what I wanted, regardless of my commitment to Him. But true faith is trusting that God knows best, and then stepping out in faith to follow wherever He leads. I was such a hypocrite, because I expected Him to meet what I perceived were *my needs*, without being willing to give Him all of myself for *His purposes*. I was a seasonal Christian, following God when it suited my desires, and *not* following when it *didn't*. In my lack of faith, I sinned, and sinned because I chose to.

With my tail between my legs, I gathered what few belongings I had and escaped once again by the skin of my teeth, going to Charlie and Laura's house in Pennsylvania. During my time living there, I would learn a new concept of what family is all about, a concept of which I knew little. This would bring to the surface many deeply buried feelings, such as holding people and the world in contempt for having families, envying people who have families, and being angry at people who have families, all because my own family had vanished in my childhood, leaving me without one.

8

A Fresh Start

Family—a New Perspective

BEFORE MY PARENTS' divorce I had a family—a mother, father, sister, and brother, living together like any normal family. There were birthdays that were celebrated as well as holidays. These were times of being together and great enjoyment. Christmas was delightful. Mom and Dad always had gifts under the tree. I remember my siblings and me enjoying coming down the stairs with sparkles in our eyes to the array of gifts Santa Claus left us the night before. I remember being hardly able to fall asleep the night before, and looking out the window to try and see the fat man in red, with a fluffy white beard, riding his sleigh pulled by the reindeer and Rudolph. Before going to sleep, we would watch Christmas shows such as *Frosty the Snowman*, *Rudolph the Red-nosed Reindeer*, and many others. We always left Santa Claus cookies and milk on the table as a gift from us.

Needless to say I never saw the jolly old elf during those long evenings, but my parents had a remedy for this. A family tradition of the pre-Christmas season was to bring us to see him at Jordan's Toy Land in Boston. For us children there was always an air of great excitement that accompanied this special occasion. Jordan's Toy Land was filled with bright colored ornaments hanging from the ceiling, a large variety of Christmas trees, and elves flittering about the store. Waiting in line with anticipation, you could see in the distance a large chair fit for a king. Surrounding the chair were brilliant white cotton balls and paper cutouts depicting snowflakes. Sitting in the chair was a large man dressed in a bright red suit. Around his belly was a large black belt with a huge gold buckle. And of course he had a great white beard as large as a small cloud. With great excitement and anticipation, I watched the line get shorter until it was my turn to talk to Santa. Running to the chair, flying like a freshly made snowball, I would splatter on his lap. Looking at his great white beard and glittering eyes, I would proceed to give him my long list of requests. This for me was and still is a great memory regarding the family and the activities surrounding a family.

My birthdays were always exciting as well. My friends would be invited, and there was a great celebration. Other holidays were also of great enjoyment, and I remember them well. As you can see, I did have a few years of experiencing some of the joys of family life. But the memories of abuse, abandonment, rejection, and the breakup of my family resonated and weighed more heavily on my heart in the days since those things happened, greatly influencing my feelings.

Over the years, the happy feelings accompanying the experience of good times with family faded because of the choices made and their consequences after my parents' divorce. First, I had no choice of family regarding living with my abusive relatives in Boston. It was an order, which I had to abide by. Second, I eventually experienced new and darker types of family—the family of drugs, sex, money, and dysfunction. As I grew older, chained to these types of families, I often chose to live alone. Alone as a way of isolating myself from those who might cause me pain. Alone on the floor surrounded by walls I built to protect my heart. Alone with negative feelings that eventually would take the place of any good memories, and even cause events such as Christmas and birthdays to bring me down into depression. Although I became a Christian, I did not realize that I still lived surrounded by walls. This would change when I moved in with Charlie and Laura and their kids, Susanne and Matthew.

Moving in with the Winkelmans allowed me to learn and experience what family is really about. I am not going to say that they were the perfect family, but what I learned was how a family acts in imperfection, by accepting imperfection and seeking to love. Eating dinner together was a different experience. Sharing space took on a new meaning. I saw how a mother nurtures the family members even when it is emotionally difficult. I saw how a father can struggle with balancing work, family, and relaxation. But mostly I saw how different family members do not ostracize one another because of inconvenience or behavioral issues. On the contrary, working things out through acceptance was a high ethic and a rigorous practice.

As I moved in, the Winkelmans accepted me also. I am not going to say that I did not challenge them, but I will say that because of this challenge all the family members gained a degree of perspective regarding the uniqueness that comes from God. Therefore they never ran away from me, although at times they may have wanted to!

An added delight was spending time with Laura's extended family, who lived near Boston. Visits with her parents Don and Doris, their grandchildren, and Laura's siblings brought additional perspectives on family. A while back I went with Laura to their home in Sudbury, Massachusetts. Charlie and Laura's son, Matthew, was researching colleges to attend. During our stay, the family celebrated birthdays. With great joy I was invited to this festive occasion. Sitting around in the family room we all shared—with bright eyes each shared the gifts that were given and what was said on the cards that were attached. Throughout this time there was laughter accompanied by jovial interaction. Experiencing this was exciting and triggered the good feelings that had accompanied some of my birthdays in the past. But most of all, it showed me love experienced in the oneness of a Christian family. This experience was one of many I had with the Winkelman and Soulé families.

What I learned the most from these experiences was God's perspective on family. I saw this from the family members in their actions, as they attempted to live out the things God prescribed for families in His word, and as He tested their faith and mine. To this day I have a place I can always call home, a place to stay if I need to, a family to enjoy life with, and a special place of rest and acceptance. I find it always a delight to commune with Charlie, Laura, Susanne, and Matthew Winkelman, and Don and Doris Soulé, a very special family, and to enjoy the acceptance from their extended family and friends such as Dan Olsen; I cannot forget Dan the Man!

College—a New Career

During my stay with the Winkelmans, Laura suggested to me that I should think about going to college and getting a degree. "A degree in what?" I asked her. In response, she said she did not know either. However, through a series of conversations with Charlie and others, it was suggested that I should attend college to become a social worker. Taking this advice, I enrolled full time at Lock Haven University in their social work program and moved into a small apartment in Lock Haven, about fifteen minutes down the road from Jersey Shore. For the next four years I attended this college and successfully graduated with a BA in social work.

Let me share my experience in academia. First, I want to tell you how some others viewed my endeavor. After graduation *many* people told me that they thought I would never graduate and they were astonished when I did! Secondly, we need to go back to my years in high school to gain perspective. While attending Quincy Vo-Tech and High School, there were many days when I went to school stoned. I was a drug dealer, and I did not care about my grades. The last year of school I missed close to seventy days. I was a full-blown drug addict and was taking the drugs known as acid, purple haze, and THC, as well as smoking pot. Smoking pot in most cases was a daily event.

My high school day started by meeting in the hole (a place in the basement of the building) to deal or buy logs, or joints. This was followed by striking up the logs and getting fired up or wasted. The hole was surrounded by four stone walls, which were painted blue. It was like being in a big fireplace. The doors were made of steel and had locks and chains on them to keep us out. Since most of us could pick locks, we were able to get access. Adjacent to the entrance doors there were four additional doors, which connected to the staircase that led up to our classrooms on the other floors. The stairway was like a chimney going up from the fireplace. Connected to the hallways were other hallways, which were like additional flues, connecting to other rooms. As smoke would rise up a chimney from the fireplace, many of us would do the same in these hallways. Going to homeroom I would drift into my classroom from the basement (fireplace), up the chimney like smoke. Floating like a puff of smoke, stinking like pot, I would hover at my desk for roll call. The following parts of the day would be a series of opportunities to again smoke pot, and on many occasions as a senior to pop acid and trip my brains out. So you can imagine how little I learned. I graduated by the skin of my teeth with very poor grades, and on top of this, I had very little recollection of what was taught in math, English, history, science, and other courses.

It was the fall of 2005 when I entered my first college class, my first trip into a classroom since 1977! With a backpack full of books, I entered the room with high anxiety. But at least high anxiety was better than high on some drug! Looking around, I saw young adults, all young enough to be my children. With great enthusiasm, I prepared myself to be taught. I do not remember what my first class was, but what I *do* remember is that I did not know *nearly* as much as my fellow students knew regarding what they had learned during their high school education.

My high school education was all a big smoke cloud that disappeared into the sky. During my college experience, every text book for every class in most cases I had to read twice. Starting early in the morning, through the day and into the evenings with a dictionary in hand, I painstakingly read my text using the dictionary to understand the words. It was as if I was going through high school all over again. So you can imagine how much effort and time I needed to exert for my studies. I was very fortunate to have a friend in Charlie who was much more educated than I was. Throughout my college experience, Charlie was a big supporter as well as a great teacher.

As school went on, I found myself reading and researching other texts, besides the ones required for my classes, which were found in the library. I did this to gain more understanding. The texts in the library were older, and in my experience, I found them to be filled with writings that seemed more understandable. I spent many hours in the library.

As the days went on, I found that I had disabilities. These involved my racing thoughts, as well as difficulty writing. Let me explain. In many cases, my brain was going so fast that what I wanted to put on paper came out garbled. Furthermore, what I was trying to write was always of large quantity, containing many ideas. Maintaining focus on one topic was difficult. I would take one topic and expand on it like a freeway going fast that entered many exits leading to many other roads.

Staying on the freeway was difficult. Added to this was my inability to retain or remember information. It seems I had long-term memory, but my short-term memory was not very functional. Because of this, what I learned from one semester did not sink in till the next semester! Understanding and applying grammar was also very difficult. (You should see what this book looked like before my friend Charlie edited it!) All the school learning from my younger years was up in smoke. (If anyone says that drugs do not affect one's memory, it's a big lie!) My drug use destroyed my short-term memory, but through God's grace, He has restored my educational abilities a great deal, and he used the Holy Spirit, prayer, and my learning experience at college to do this.

Expanding on my long-term and short-term memory issues, this situation actually worked out for the good with regard to my major in social work. Social work required me to do a great deal of practical application. This was shared with the class by giving PowerPoint presentations regarding research on social problems, understanding of human behavior, and the application of counseling, diversity, policy, and disease, which I read from many texts, but which I had also learned from the many different experiences in my past. God used my disability in this way: whenever I gave a presentation, I was able to present information right from my long-term memory. It was like building a house, starting with the foundation and building up from there. In most cases, I did not have to read off the PowerPoint, which many students did, but instead pulled questions from my PowerPoint, which triggered my memory, and made my presentation sound very professional. "God works in mysterious ways is wonders to perform!"[1]

God also used my experience in college to help me reflect on myself. He used my professors as well as my texts to help me recognize the many areas of my life that still needed healing, bringing me to the cross with them for closure. As you can see from my story, my life has been a social worker's dream in terms of the types of experiences I have had that are also the focus of social work. My experiences certainly helped inform my understanding of social work, but my college education in social work also helped me understand better my experiences. Through every page and chapter of my textbooks, it was as if I was reading about the different parts of my life! The process brought a great deal of discouragement as I relived the various emotions and regrets. But it also brought encouragement as I learned I was not alone in my struggles, and my own experiences could provide valuable knowledge for helping others.

---

[1] Allusion to a 1779 hymn by William Cowper, friend of John Newton and hymn writer who also struggled with depression!

College for me was very enlightening. I learned about this younger generation, about the different generations of my professors, and about various social theories and statistics. But most of all, I learned how God can use my past trials and tribulations to help people, especially youth. I learned the greatness of how God can rebuild from and through brokenness into oneness.

It was a warm spring day in May 2009 when I experienced the thrill of finally being able to graduate from college! I assure you all of my teachers from high school would never have thought that was even a possibility for me! As I stood getting my photo taken after the ceremony, holding my diploma, with my daughter standing beside me smiling, I couldn't wait for all the wonderful things I would be able to do. Once again, however, God had a few curveballs waiting for me!

9

Surviving Losses

The Loss of Employment

IT TOOK SOME months of job searching, given the poor economy, but I was finally hired as a case worker by an agency called CASA (Court Appointed Special Advocates) hosted by the YWCA in Williamsport, PA. My job was to help the special advocates and families of juveniles in trouble to navigate the courts and legal system. Although there was not much direct working with kids, as I would have preferred, I jumped into my new job with enthusiasm. Because of my background and schooling, I was uniquely equipped to understand what these young people and families were dealing with. I received much praise and appreciation from the advocates and families I worked with, and affirmation from my supervisor. Finally God was using my background and work to help people, and I had a new sense of purpose!

Alas, it was not to last. The supervisor who had hired me moved on to another job. My new supervisor and I did not see eye to eye. My political naiveté and propensity to bluntly tell the truth as I saw it probably did not help me any. After nine months of fruitful labor, I suddenly found myself out of a job. The official reason given was that my grammar in written reports was not up to professional standards. That was no doubt an accurate statement, but I had my doubts it was the real reason. I will refrain from saying more than that! Although I was trusting God, my new sense of purpose definitely took a hit.

It was now the summer of 2010. My friend Charlie took a group of teens on a week-long mission trip to Maine to do home repair for low income folks, and I went along as one of the leaders. The work went fine, but as usual, I overdid it physically and experienced a lot of pain. At the end of the week, we were scheduled to go on a whitewater rafting trip on the Kennebec River. Feeling the pain of the week, I decided not to go. Charlie said he needed me to help drive. A huge argument followed, and I ended up going. We had a great time on the river, although it did increase my pain. But the real problem was the damage done to my relationship with Charlie. Although we came back still friends, it felt more distant than before.

That fall I was invited to a men's Bible study by a pastor friend Charlie and I had worked with on joint youth events, Tom Seaman. Tom was in the process of helping a new church get started, and I felt drawn to help them out. At my invitation, Charlie started attending the Bible study also. After awhile some members of the group decided to break off and form *another* new church. Tom was part of the first group, and I began to lead a men's study for the second group, which was seeking a pastor. I made some new friends and also started bringing my "little," Malcom, and his sister to church. But I missed my friendships at Jersey Shore and still had no gainful employment, surviving only on my disability check from my previous injuries.

The Loss of Sobriety

I began to sink into a depression. I also was not taking my bipolar medication on a regular schedule, but only when I felt I needed it. This is a classic and frequent mistake made by people with bipolar disorder. I spent a lot of time in my dark apartment playing video games and watching movies on my large screen TV. To top it all off, Malcom and his family moved to another part of the state, giving me another feeling of loss.

To get some income and pull myself up out of my funk, I did what I had done before—I started a new electrical and construction business with a partner. As we began to get more business, I pushed myself physically to keep up with my younger partner and my own perfectionist standards. My pain levels increased, and with no regular bipolar medicine, I began to abuse my pain medication. I also got a prescription for the anxiety drug Xanax, which turned out to be a *very* bad combination with my other medications. In manic periods I also hit the crack pipe again and would lose whole days in a row.

Everything came to a head in November of 2011. My daughter found me passed out on my bed from an unknown combination of medicines and drugs, with some superficial cuts on my wrists. She got me to the hospital and called Charlie. Meanwhile, I somehow escaped from the hospital and walked to a local friend's house in Lock Haven. (Most of this I have been told; I remember very little of it myself). My friend drove me back to my apartment. Meanwhile, Charlie and my business partner came to my apartment, found me, and called my daughter. When she got there, I was half out of my mind, but my social work training kicked in, and I began to lead my own intervention! I explained to everyone what my alternatives were. They quickly informed me it didn't work that way. They took me to the hospital again and filled out a Form 302, committing me to treatment whether I wanted it or not. Soon the state police came by to take me to a treatment facility in Philadelphia for the next twenty-one days. Charlie contacted close friends and two churches, and lots of prayers were said for me.

At the treatment center, one major emphasis was the necessity of staying on the prescribed treatment schedule for my bipolar and pain medications. I realized that these were things the Lord intended to help me. God works through prayer and sometimes miraculous healing, but He also works through doctors and medicine.

When I was released, they told me I needed to live with someone who could help me stay accountable with my medications. So I once again moved in with Charlie and Laura. With their children in college, they had plenty of room, and it has turned out to be a real blessing in my life. I began to get involved again at the Jersey Shore Presbyterian Church, helping with the youth, a new men's Bible study, and a new After School Kids (ASK) program every Wednesday afternoon for kids from the neighborhood around the church. As it turned out, moving in with the Winkelmans was also quite providential for the next great trial I would face—the deaths of my mother and father.

The Loss of Parents

My mother from a young age was a smoker. She had always tried to quit, but to no avail. At age eighty-five it caught up with her. In February of 2012 she was diagnosed with stage 4 lung cancer, giving her only months to live. But the Lord had started preparing me for her death a few years before that with a strange dream.

In the dream, I was taken up into heaven. I was called up there by an angel, and as I was rising up, I saw below me my sister Donna, my brother Neal, and my mom. My mom said, "Tell God to remember me." Rising higher I saw a great tunnel full of light and clouds, with a greater light at the end. The light flickered, and within a moment, I woke up. I felt a sense of both awe and concern—awe for God and concern for my mom.

Then in September of 2011, when I was starting to spiral downward again, the Holy Spirit prompted me with a burden for my mom. The Spirit told me there was something wrong with her and I needed to tell Charlie and ask for prayers for her, which I did. I continued to be prompted and mentioned to Charlie that I felt she was going to die. Then in February she was diagnosed.

Meanwhile my sister Donna was also receiving some heavenly communication. She had a pregnant friend who was concerned about her unborn child because she was having complications. God gave a revelation to Donna, which she passed along to her friend: "The baby will be born after my mom dies, and will be healthy." As it turned out, my mom died on Thursday, April 19, 2012, and the baby was born premature but healthy with no complications a few days later!

Early in February, after the diagnosis, my daughter and I traveled down to Virginia to visit my mom and family.

Mom looked good but was feeling a bit down, but we just loved on her and had a great visit.

Later in February, Mom took a turn for the worse. She was being admitted to a hospice for her final months. I planned another trip down to spend a week with Mom, being joined by my daughter on the weekend. It did not work out like this. Meeting my sister at my mom's apartment, I came in and saw Mom back in the bed. She looked frail and sucked in. This took me on a whirlwind for the next three days. I only remember bits and pieces. Apparently I took an anxiety pill similar to Xanax, which took me down. It was awful. I completely messed up on taking my medications, got into a fender-bender, and was totally out of it. Four days later I drove home to Jersey Shore with my tail between my legs. I had only spent a brief afternoon with Mom. I have failed many times before in my life, but this was the worst.

Lying in my bed when I got home, I reached up and closed the curtain. Depressed, disappointed, and suicidal, all I could think of was how much of a heel I was. Charlie came into the back bedroom they had given me and comforted me, saying he loved me. That was fine, but did my *mom* love me? This failure tore into my soul, bringing to the surface from my past all the feelings of not being loved by Mom. My whole life I had blamed her and Dad for abandoning me. I had felt unloved, and that I was a nobody because of them.

The week Mom died, I had an experience that finally brought me peace. I shared this experience at her memorial service, not without a few tears. Here's what I said:

God's Love and Mom's Love

I'd like to share with you a familiar but powerful verse about God's love that saved my mom and me. In John 3:16–17, Jesus says, "For God so loved the world that He gave His only Son, that whoever believes in Him should not perish but have eternal life. For God did not send His Son into the world to *condemn* the world, but in order that the world might be saved through Him." Whoever believes in Him is not condemned.

Like God, Mom loved me although I was a wretched son. Mom loved me by praying for me. All the time! Mom's prayers led me to accepting Christ! Mom loves me even though I am *still* a wretched son! There have been people who have not loved me. However, God still loves me, enough to die for me. And Mom still loves me.

She showed me this and taught me this while she was dying. The week she died, I was trying to call her but was not getting through for various reasons. Finally we got connected. I told her I loved her, and I will miss her. Although unable to speak, somehow she spoke to my heart and told me she loves me and forgives me! A half hour after this, Mom died. She had waited for me to call her! She hung on to life until I called, waiting to tell me this. I will miss my mom, but I look forward to seeing her in heaven.

I share this last experience with you. When I was at the funeral home last night and looked at Mom, it was as if she looked at me and grabbed my hand for the last time in this world, and then went to heaven. It was as if she waited again to be there with me to see me, and to make sure I was okay. And then I was at peace. I often failed Mom as a son. But *she* did not fail *me*. I have often failed the Lord as *His* son. But He too has never failed *me*. Today I am so thankful for their love, and that they are together, in heaven.

After the funeral, my sister, brother, and I met that evening to have dinner, along with Charlie, who had come down to Virginia with me for the funeral. After a hearty meal at Chi Chi's, Donna was able to share her feelings. Over the years she had carried a great deal of baggage, such as I did. She reflected on how she had become, at age thirteen, a caretaker for me and Neal, while Mom was out partying with the neighbors. Many days Donna was the one who made sure Neal and I were safely tucked away in bed. This happened both before and after our parents' divorce. Donna would stay up late into the evening, waiting for Mom to come home, only to be disappointed when she did. Many times they would get into arguments. One time Donna told her what she was doing wasn't right. Reeking of booze, Mom asked her who was *she* to tell *her* what to do? These many moments weighed heavily on my sister's heart over the years and into the last three months of my mother's life, when my sister became her caregiver. Donna realized she had a deep resentment toward Mom, such as the one I had for both our parents. The memory of these stormy moments and times had cast a shadow over Donna, Neal, and me, as we were led astray into the darkness of our lives in the future.

That night at the restaurant, however, Donna shared through her tears about a miracle. One day, toward the end, Mom had rallied enough to ask Donna a question. In a weak voice breaking with emotion, she asked Donna, "Can you forgive me?"

Donna's heart melted as she responded, "I *do* forgive you, Mom." Then Donna added, "Will *you* forgive *me*?"

Mom responded, "For what?"

She no doubt knew of Donna's resentment, but had already forgiven and forgotten it. This simple story of forgiveness brought me and my siblings closer together than we had been in years, as we shared with each other the feelings of abandonment and loneliness we had each experienced. Our mom had always wanted and prayed for our family to be back together again. In the aftermath of her death, as she herself was experiencing that amazing reconciliation with her Lord in the hallowed halls of heaven, Jesus answered her prayer!

Within three months, my father also died. But not before a talk with him that confirmed his faith in the Lord. It was a rough year for me. But through it all, Christ was loving me, bringing me further from brokenness into His oneness, a journey that will continue until I see Him face to face in Heaven.

Since Then

Since that year, things have gone better. I've still had some struggles, but God has brought me through every one. My bipolar swings have been less severe as I've taken my medication, and just recently, I went through detox and treatment to get off of opioid pain medication completely. My work at church with the youth has produced much fruit, and I have been able to preach a number of times when Charlie had to be away. I've also been able to serve as an elder, help the church on their maintenance committee, and start a men's Bible study group. I've reduced my electrical work to half days, and this coming fall (2016), I hope to begin a master's degree program in mental health counseling at a local college. My fellowship with the Lord early each morning has both challenged me greatly and inspired me deeply. For all of this, I give all glory to God my Father, and my Lord, Jesus Christ, who through the power of His Holy Spirit continues to bring me from brokenness into oneness.

10

Looking Back

Feelings of Loneliness versus Solitude

THROUGHOUT MY LIFE I have wandered in this world, surrounded by many people, and yet felt loneliness. I was always searching. What was I searching for? Searching to not have these feelings of loneliness! All my searches came to dead ends—dead end in companionship, dead end in people, dead end in business, dead end in marriage, and dead end in anything that had to do with people, places, and things. All the hoped for "solutions" were temporary and fleeting. Today as a Christian, *loneliness* has faded away to the point that now I generally only experience *being alone* (solitude). There is a difference between the two, and this difference can be understood from the teaching of the

Holy Spirit, whose indwelling presence for the Christian means that we are never completely alone.

In many cases, religious groups as well as people have misunderstood me and also my diagnoses, and therefore I was ostracized. I believe this was often due to ignorance, such as people who felt threatened by my having HIV or being bipolar. Even though this happened, and consumed me in some cases, God used the process to help me understand why. One could say it is a paradox. The ways of the Lord are *not* the ways of the world. The world teaches that to relieve loneliness one must receive acceptance and be with a group or person. However, it is not by *receiving* from groups or people, or *being* accepted, but by giving and accepting *them* that loneliness is relieved! God showed me my ignorance and my hypocrisy regarding this. But acceptance is still something I battle with.

Christ in many ways was misunderstood and ostracized by religious groups and people, and even by His own nation, which rejected him. As He lived in this world, His lonely feelings far outweighed anything I have ever experienced. As Isaiah foresaw, He was "a man of sorrows, and acquainted with grief."[1] Though He never sinned, He was broken! When He descended into hell for three days and especially when He took our sins in His body on the cross and cried out, "My God, my God, why have you forsaken me?" it was

---

[1]   Isaiah 53:3

the moment of Him being extremely alone.[2] This happened when He was separated from His Father by our sins. I can say that when I feel separated in any way from my Heavenly Father, that is when I feel lonely as a Christian, separated because of my sins. Before I accepted Christ, in my lowest moment, is when I felt the most loneliness and despair. As I grow in Christ, I have learned that there are many areas of my past life that make me feel this. Today, because of my various conditions and behaviors and past experiences, as I said before, many people have misunderstood me. So I try to put into practice what Jesus has taught me. Above all, He has taught me to love and understand people and groups who may not accept me, or who see me as a loser. Therefore the supremacy of God's truth from His word and His wisdom in this matter defuses and helps me rise above, and not feel loneliness, but merely being alone (in solitude with God)—from brokenness into oneness.

Nobody Wants Anything to Do with "Losers"

We live in a society that shuns people who appear to be losers. Alcoholics, drug addicts, prostitutes, people who are diseased, people who are different, people who are poor, people who are a product of choices they made, or choices others made for them, people of the world. If we look, we

---

[2]   See 1 Peter 2:24 and Matthew 27:46.

can find them in our backyards, across the street, and in our communities. These so-called losers are people who feel alone and are searching for an identity. It is sad to say some have found their identity in things that have destroyed them.

But if we flip the coin, so-called losers are not necessarily characterized by what I wrote. You could say, so to speak, that losers can be from higher class societies as well, people of wealth or prominence, people from a higher status, who also search for identity. So what does the word *loser* mean? If you look in the Bible, you will not find the word *loser* used to define anyone. The word *loser* is a word of ignorance. This powerful word has cut the heart and the very being of many people, both poor and rich, and has caused feelings of loneliness.

Speaking of my own experience, I had for the longest time seen myself as a loser. A loser because people have defined me using this word, either by what I did or did not do. A loser because of my actions, my beliefs, my education, my upbringing, my poverty, my grammar, my looks, or my nationality. Of course this has not always been the case. At times when things were going well for me as a Christian and I had plenty, I was stamped a winner. But even as a Christian I have often been stamped a loser by many groups, both secular and religious. Sadly, many are external thinkers and only see the tangible.

My feelings of being a loser represent the down times of an ongoing internal battle between how I see myself and how Jesus sees me. But as I explained before, this has helped me understand more about myself and the word of God. I realized I was a people pleaser and took more stock in people's opinions than in Jesus' attitude and acceptance of me.

When Jesus walked this earth, He saw beyond this word *loser*—He accepted all! He saw the brokenness in people's hearts, and therefore He felt compassion. He felt compassion for the alcoholics, drug addicts, prostitutes, people who were diseased, people who were different, people who were poor, people who were a product of choices they made, or choices others made for them, the rich, the tax collectors, the lepers, even the hypocritical religious leaders, and all people of all nations. He showed this by preaching and acting in love, and teaching how we are lost children of God whom He longs to welcome home.[3] It is sad today that love is not expressed *more* by people who have accepted Christ stepping out of their comfort zone, by people who are Christians, who should be acting with genuine love, and not condemnation. It is safe to say the only way to combat people being stamped loser is by the word of God through Jesus Christ, and not by the word of man—*loser!* The worth of something is determined by the purpose of the one who created it and what price someone will pay for it. God's word declares we were created in His image to be His representatives, and redeemed from sin and death

---

[3]   See Luke 15:11–32.

by the priceless blood of His Son. This gives each of us infinite worth!

Today in my life I still have a small degree of this feeling of being a loser; past hurts are not yet completely healed. But most of the time I feel as if I am a winner, because I am not guided by what my earthly father called me or how people view me. Today I am guided by the Holy Spirit, His word, and His fruit of love, joy, peace, patience, kindness, goodness, gentleness, faithfulness, and self-control.[4] I am able to pass along this blessing to the youth and children I minister to each week. I am reassured most of all by how God my Heavenly Father through Jesus Christ views me—as His child, a saint, a conqueror[5], and a man who has been taken from hell's loneliness into God's heavenly family. Brokenness into oneness!

Why the World Thinks It Does Not Need God/Jesus

Throughout history, mankind has often seen no need for God. This is especially true today in America. One can understand why. We have been blessed with abundance. Many social problems, in the eyes of society, have seen improvement, according to research. Homes, cars, and materialistic items, even in the midst of economic turmoil and high

---

[4]   See Galatians 5:22–23.

[5]   See John 1:12, 1 Corinthians 1:2, and Romans 8:31–39.

unemployment, are at the fingertips of most. We have pills and procedures to take away depression, disease, disability, and dimples. People today, in comparison to yesterday, are living longer lives in better conditions. Problems such as terrorism, natural disasters, the national debt, teen pregnancy, and drug cartels cause concern, but there are a wide array of government and social agencies claiming to have solutions.

With all of this available, why do we need God or Jesus? What a conundrum—tangibles versus faith! Why deal with the conditions of the heart when you can escape from them by popping a pill, drinking alcohol, having sex, going shopping, spending money, watching pornography, playing a video game, getting on Facebook, having multiple relationships, or just about anything? At one time I myself believed these would take away the deepest troubles of my heart. These are the things in my life I had to be broken from. In my personal experience, these are all a dead end, and something one often uses to replace the true God. At the end, we all will be held accountable. The time will come when all the things of the world will fade. What will be left is your heart and God. This is all the more reason we need God and Jesus now.

Why the World Actually *Does* Need God/Jesus

Jesus died on the cross for all who accept Him. In this is faith, hope, and freedom, brokenness into oneness. In my life I have lived in the pit of hell. Before I was saved, I never *knew* I was living in it. Jesus brought truth into my life, giving me a new and powerful perspective. For the first time, I saw how the things of the world could not save me but only lead me deeper into bondage. The only Savior is Jesus Himself. Trusting in Him and surrendering my life to His direction is the only way to receive salvation.

This is more than just a one-time decision. It still goes on for me today. He brings perspective as His truth breaks the chains on my heart, the fog of denial vanishes, and He brings me out from the pit of hell. I have many logs in my eye, logs of sin that keep me from seeing life correctly (see Scripture below). If these logs are not removed by God/ Jesus, I remain in denial, not even seeing that I *have* a problem! The good news is that God's Son gives us life! I am a vile sinner. His truth and blood set me free. Slowly I now can see a little more clearly.

> Judge not, that you be not judged. For with the judgment you pronounce you will be judged, and the measure you use it will be measured to you. Why do you see the speck that is in your brother's eye, but do not notice the log that is in your own eye? Or how can you say to your brother, "Let me take the speck out of your eye," when there is the log in your own eye? (Matt. 7:1–3)

This is why the world needs God/Jesus. I have described the many things I did, and how the pleasure from them was fleeting. I remember how I felt after I indulged in them. At first it was fine, but it only kept me seeking, indulging, and therefore becoming bound. At the end of each there was just me, my heart, and the many feelings I had not dealt with. I felt like a wet loaf of bread.

Even people who are blessed with being rich have times when they question their feelings of despair and feel like a wet loaf of bread. History has stories of many people who struggled with this, finding themselves in the conundrum of tangibles versus faith, at times even to the point of taking their own life.

> And behold, a man came up to him, saying, "Teacher, what good deed must I do to have eternal life?" And he said to him, "… If you would enter life, keep the commandments." He said to him, "Which ones?" And Jesus said, "You shall not murder, You shall not commit adultery, ou shall not steal, ou shall not bear false witness, Honor your father and mother, and, ou shall love your neighbor as yourself." The young man said to him, "All these I have kept. What do I still lack?" Jesus said to him, "If you would be perfect, go, sell what you possess and give to the poor, and you will have treasure in heaven; and come, follow me." When the young man heard this he went away sorrowful, for he had great possessions. And Jesus said to his disciples, "Truly, I say to you, only with difficulty will a rich person enter the kingdom of heaven." (Matt. 19:16–23)

I have heard a quote, "A rich man's biggest fear is being poor." I suspect this is true for most. Even Jesus said it is harder for a rich man to enter the kingdom of heaven than for a camel to go through the eye of a needle. Many think poverty cannot happen. But remember the Great Depression!

> Listen, my beloved brothers, has not God chosen those who are poor in the world to be rich in faith and heirs of the kingdom, which he has promised to those who love him? (James 2:5)

Speaking from experience, at one point in my business life, I was financially secure with riches, but they became my idol, and when I lost everything, I was broken once more. One can have the greatest intentions with wealth, but having it brings its own form of servitude. Our possessions possess us. I once spoke with a man who owned a Fortune 500 company. He said, "Eric, when you create a monster, you must feed it, and then you become the servant and it becomes your master." It is your choice what master you want! But neither riches nor anything else besides Jesus can save us!

Therefore, the world needs Jesus. Everyone. My profession and path have brought me to work with children. The horrifying acts of abuse they suffer are unspeakable. This is another reason the world needs God/Jesus. I know this because I was one of these children, a survivor of abuse and neglect. Only because of Him am I alive and dealing slowly with my past. No policy, no person, place, or thing, besides Him, can cure. My professor, Dr. Lynette Reitz, told me, "Eric, no one can change the human heart." She's right, except for Jesus. So I say, "Heed the word of God, or become a weed of the world."

Needing Jesus, and Growing to Want and Love Him

Because the tragedies in my life began so young, each one provided materials to lay the foundation of every part of my being. These foundational materials influenced the choices I made later, and the thoughts and feelings I have to this day. The deeper my relationship grows with Christ, the deeper I sense how vile a man I am, and how much I have to thank Him for in His mercy.

> In this you rejoice, though now for a little while, as was necessary, you have been grieved by various trials, so that the tested genuineness of your faith—more precious than gold that perishes though it is tested by fire—may be found to result in praise and glory and honor at the revelation of Jesus Christ. Though you have not seen him, you love him. Though you do not now see him, you believe in him and rejoice with joy that is inexpressible and filled with glory, obtaining the outcome of your faith, the salvation of your souls. (1 Pet. 1:6–9)

When I became a born-again believer, it was out of need, as well as a product of Jesus' love for me. God knew all my sins and motives, He knew everything about me, most of all He knew I needed His love and acceptance. His response to my tragedies was not to provide instant gratification, but rather seasoned sanctification. Through this, as I matured, I learned how to *want* to love Him, and how I fell short whenever I tried to use my arsenal of methods to escape my past. What I learned is that no matter what happened to me, both then and now, God loves me and daily fills me with the revitalizing presence of the Holy Spirit. Before the world was even created, He chose me to *want* to choose Him (Eph. 1:4), and to be a bond servant wanting to love Him with all of my heart, mind, soul, and strength.

In this first section, I have written chronologically and briefly about the tragedies in my life, and how God turned these occasions of brokenness into oneness with Him. In the second section, I will delve into some of these experiences in a deeper, more topical manner, showing how God turned brokenness into oneness in each area. My hope is that this will be helpful to those struggling in specific areas. Some details of stories already shared may be repeated in certain chapters for the sake of completeness for those turning to a chapter for reference.

I end this section with this: It was by my own hand and sin that my path was set. But through Christ's death in my place, my repentance and trust in Him, and His forgiveness, there is accountability for my actions. His action of forgiveness brings forth forgiveness in me, so I do not blame my conditions on those who hurt me, and with this comes freedom.

It is easy to have faith when life brings soft breezes of pleasure. But faith does not increase from pleasure. On the contrary, faith is best produced when life brings storms of tribulation. In those storms, we are tempted to see ourselves as victims, to which I succumbed for a season. It is God's absolute truth that brings forth the fact that we live in sin and are sinners, from the day we are born to the day we die. In this sin, there will be a variety of storms in life. But when we have a relationship with Christ, He uses these to produce the power of genuine love, empathy, and compassion for others.

If God is tugging at your heart right now, I want you to know that you can have salvation and a relationship with Him through His Son, Jesus Christ, and you can have it right now! Turn to chapter 26 where I will tell you how.

PART II

AREAS OF BROKENNESS AND ONENESS

The list of problems I have faced in my life reads like a catalog of personal and social issues so many are struggling with today: abuse, broken families, abandonment, addictions, grief, life-threatening disease, chronic pain, sexual sin, mental illness, and the loss of all. In part 2, I look at each of these areas of brokenness in separate chapters that discuss the root causes, how the problem affected my life, the method(s) God used to heal that area of brokenness, and where a person struggling with that problem can turn for help. Some details of stories shared in Part I may be repeated in the following chapters for the sake of completeness for those referencing these chapters.

11

Brokenness from Abuse

Into Oneness through Forgiveness

I REMEMBER RUNNING around in a scurry of panic as my father chased me. With every raising of his hand I could see the strap ready to lay into my skin. My mind in deep turmoil, my heart racing, I barely heard him say the longer I kept moving, the longer this would last. Glancing back, I saw the anger in his face matched the anger in his voice. Inevitably, I lost the race. After the beating, I would lie exhausted and hurting on my bed, crying. Sometimes he would force me into the closet, shutting the door behind me. A multitude of welts marked my body. In a pool of tears, I learned to accept these beatings as "the way things are." I don't doubt that I often needed discipline, but I now know this was clearly over the line. As I lay on my bed, I would hear my sister and mother crying. Rising after an hour or so, I would go downstairs where my mother would try to console me. For the next few weeks, I would feel the sour fruit from these beatings. I won't say it was every day, because I cannot recall. In my memory today, it seems a blur—they were all the same.

This chapter is for all who have been abused and suffer from the fallout. Perhaps you will see yourself, or a loved one, in some of these stories. Let me tell you that there is hope! I will tell you how at the end of the chapter, but first let me share a closer look at some of the things I experienced. Perhaps you can relate.

Wandering into the horizon of the railroad tracks one day, I found a mud hole to play in. Back in the distance I heard my name being called. Checking to see who was calling, I saw my mom, with fear and anger in her eyes. She grabbed me and dragged me home, only to have me go back outside to find a switch, which she used to lay into me. (I had to learn well how to choose the stick, because if I chose one too small, she would go out and find one she thought was a more appropriate size! Choosing a medium stick was smart on my end—no pun intended.) I was often on the receiving end of her frustration and anger at my father.

Tuesday was my father's day off. It was like walking on eggshells at home. My mother always tried to keep us quiet by sending us outside. Eventually my father would rise to do chores around the house. With this I always tensed up, because now I became his little servant. My task master was not gracious, and serving him was hard. We had a basement where there was a workbench. My father's projects always started here. He would fix a door or work on another project, but what he worked on the most was me. I became his gopher. Go for this, go get that. This was fine, until I could not find something. Then a loud voice would tear into my emotions.

The voice made me feel worthless and confused. It said things like, "You will never amount to anything!" and "Dummy!" which tore through my heart. I could never please my father. Only in the last few years have I been able to deal with the haunting memory of that voice and the hurtful words he said. Words are strong. I do not know which were worse, the words or the beatings. I suspect it was the words. Mental welts last longer.

I do not remember the day or year—I believe I was around the age of nine. Like usual after school, I and a friend (who happened to be a girl) were playing around the neighborhood. But this day we did more than play. Down the road from my house was a stone cutter's shop. Around the building were large monuments. But on this day, lurking in the background was an older boy.

This boy, in his late teens but still living at home in our neighborhood, confronted my girl friend and me. Over the next couple days, he would spend some time being our friend. But friendship was far from his intentions. In the back of his mind, he was setting us up to be sexually molested. As we met, he molested me. This went on for moments each day for a few days, until my girl friend brought it to her mother's attention. With this happening, my parents would soon find out.

Find out they did. But it was what they did *not* do that affected me. My parents did nothing! Perhaps they were afraid of a racial reaction by the neighbors, since the boy was Italian. Again, I accepted the abuse, but what hurt most of all was my parents not doing anything. My feelings surfaced, saying, "If they love me, why did they do nothing?" As I mentioned before, this led to suicidal thoughts and eventually an attempt, the first of several in my life.

Saturdays would come soon after a hard week at school. This is when I would go to work for my dad. At first I looked forward to working at my father's Chinese restaurant. He was a gourmet chef, and I eventually learned to cook some tasty meals by observing him, which I enjoy doing to this day. As I said earlier, my father decided it would be a good idea for me to learn the value of a dollar. So at the age of ten or eleven, I learned how to work hard washing dishes and being a busboy.

The restaurant was located in Newton, Massachusetts. My father was highly respected in the Chinese community, and having been in business before, he soon found success. This would not be the case for me. What I learned was to work hard, get paid less than others, and endure the abuse from the cooks.

Out of the kitchen would come a scream. My father and one of his partners would come into the kitchen. Standing there, my father would see me with tears rolling down from my eyes, and ask, "What happened?"

"Father, the cooks are pinching me and it hurts!" Looking at his friends, he would ask them what happened. They explained they were just joking around. Then he would console them, and tell them not to worry, followed by telling me it was not all that bad. It was bad all right, bad enough to leave twisted bruises on my body.

Again I accepted the abuse and the twisted bruised skin over a long time, but what I had a hard time with was why my father did nothing again? As time moved on, my father moved on as well, leaving the restaurant business, but this happened only after my parents' divorce.

As a child, I experienced a wide range of abuse, including physical beatings, verbal abuse, sexual molestation, neglect, starvation, abandonment, and being treated like a dog. The question that burned in me, that arises in the heart of anyone who has been abused, is, "Why? Why was I abused?" Often we blame ourselves ("If I was a better son, it wouldn't happen"). But that is not the reason. I was abused because of the cycle of sin. The Bible says that the sins of the father (and their consequences) are visited on the children to the third and fourth generations. This started in the Garden of Eden. My father had suffered as a child, and he ended up passing that on to me.

The other question is, how have I been able to rise above the fallout of abuse? It was *not* by anything that *I* have done! It has *only* been through the love and forgiveness that are found in Jesus Christ! As I accepted His love and forgiveness through the cross, He has built my relationship with Him. A *deep relentless peace* comes with this, a peace that you cannot buy or obtain by any earthly means. Don't get me wrong, I still experience periods of confusion from the bad memories I have, and this has happened often—but it has lessened. In most cases, this happens when I am not following God's will. Sometimes God has to let me experience His chastisement. But His discipline is much different than that dished out by human fathers. It is gentle, though firm, and it is done out of love, for my good.[1] Confusion from chastisement is not a product of the world, it is spiritual. In God's immense love for me, He lets things happen that will eventually help me. Nothing evil comes from God, only good. Even though abuse is evil, and not *caused* by God, He can redeem it in our lives to produce great good. The Bible says that God works *all things* to the good for those who love Him and are called according to His purpose (Rom. 8:28).

I think it is important that we also understand the role of Satan and demons. Beyond any comprehension, I am absolutely certain there is a war going on between good and evil, one I cannot see but only feel. This is spiritual

---

[1]   See Hebrews 12:5–11.

warfare. Satan is extremely smart, and I have learned not to underestimate his powers. He is the best magician in using illusion, the illusion that comes from his invention, the lie. He knows how to attack me. For example, since I have been abused, he uses every area regarding this to manipulate me to blame God. It is not God's fault. Knowing this, we must become warriors for Christ. As His warriors, Christ tells us in Scripture to put on the full armor of God, and in love, faith, accountability, truth, and integrity to move forward with the Holy Spirit. This is done to defeat Satan's attacks, in which he uses the abuse in our past to try to draw us away from God. (For more on this topic, see chapter 25.

With all my heart, I request that whoever reads this chapter know that I have experienced two things regarding the sin of abuse. First is the selfish and shallow embodiment of the abuse, which fueled and drove me to feel the darkness that comes from hate and contempt. This nearly destroyed me. Secondly, however, through grace and love from Jesus Christ, He used these feelings to give me a spirit of brokenness so I could go on to know His oneness. In this victory, I no longer have to wallow in hurtful memories from the past but can live for the present and eternity as an ambassador for Christ, a man of God (not just an abused child who grew up to succeed).

As Christ accepted and has forgiven me, and I accepted Him, I learned a oneness with Him, like the oneness I wanted with my dad. God showed me through His oneness that I can also be one with my father as well as my mom, that is, be reconciled with them. This I have done by accepting my past and forgiving them. (For the miraculous story of how this happened with my dad, see chapter 6.) Man is sinful and has free will, and it was not by God's hand that these abuses happened. As I acted in God's will, reflecting through God's eyes, with God healing me, it brought to the surface His knowledge. This knowledge, from brokenness, enabled me to be used in working with at-risk youth. To understand the abused, one must learn from being abused, and forgiving the abusers. *Forgiveness from Christ* heals the heart and brings oneness. As my father sinned, so I was handed down his sins and their fallout, but the vicious cycle was broken when I accepted Christ Jesus into my heart and received His forgiveness, a forgiveness I could then pass on to others.

That same forgiveness from Christ can heal the wounds and bring oneness for *anyone* who has suffered abuse, and who is willing to receive Christ as Savior and Lord. But once we receive that forgiveness, it is crucial to pass it on, as difficult as that may be to do. To not forgive is to carry a burden of bitterness that will never heal! As Jesus says in the Lord's Prayer, the prayer He taught His disciples to pray, we must ask God to forgive our debts or trespasses (sins) as we also forgive the sins of those who have sinned against us.[2] Not doing so would indicate we really have not understood or received forgiveness for ourselves.

---

[2] See Matthew 6:12, 14–15.

Reconciliation is not *always* possible (for example, if the abuser has died), or even advisable (if there is a danger of further abuse). When one is being abused, it is extremely important to get help in ending or escaping the abuse (see resources below). But forgiveness is possible, and necessary, through the power of Christ, even when reconciliation is not.

Resources to Contact for Help

> Disclaimer: Not all resources listed are necessarily Christian, nor can I vouch for their quality or contact info. Do your own research before contacting, but be safe in using a computer—search information cannot always be erased.
>
> Call 9-1-1 if you are in immediate danger.
>
> Our greatest need is a relationship with Jesus! Call 1-888-NEEDHIM (633-3446)
>
> The National Domesic Violence Hotline: 1-800-799-SAFE (7233)
>
> Online lists of many types of hotlines: keepthefaith.com/page/crisis-help, yourcross.org/hotlines
>
> Focus on the Family: 1-800-AFAMILY (232-6459) or 1-855-771-HELP, focusonthefamily.com
>
> Billy Graham Association: 1-877-772-4559, billygraham.org

Grace Help Line 24 Hour Christian service 1-800-982-8032

The 700 Club Hotline 1-800-759-0700

National Sexual Assault Hotline 1-800-656-HOPE (4673)

Stop it Now! 1-888-PREVENT

United States Elder Abuse Hotline 1-866-363-4276

National Child Abuse Hotline 1-800-4-A-CHILD (422-4453)

Child Abuse National Hotline 1-800-25ABUSE

Children in immediate danger 1-800-THE-LOST

RAINN: Rape, Abuse and Incest National Network: 1-800-656-4673 (24/7), rainn.org

Friends of Battered Women and Their Children: 1-800-603-HELP (4357)

12

Brokenness from a Broken Family

Into Oneness through Serving

LATE AT NIGHT my sister and I would hear yelling and screaming in the kitchen downstairs. At first the arguments were few and far between, but as the years passed, they became more frequent. My brother was a baby at the time and did not hear them due to his deep sleep.

My father worked late into the evening causing him to arrive at home early in the morning. But one morning he did not arrive. Going downstairs, my sister and I met my mother in the kitchen. She had been up all night worrying. Her eyes were blood-shot from crying, and tears were rolling down her face. Reaching over for a hug, my mother embraced me, perhaps looking for me to console her.

I was only twelve and did not know what to do. The whole family, except my brother, was in shock. My mother asked me to go with her to Boston to my grandmother's house to see if we could find my father. We did this, but it was in vain—there was no trace of my dad there. Riding back on the train from Boston, my mother was a wreck.

My mother being a wreck was subtle compared to what happened next. Through a series of events over a period of weeks, my father confessed his unfaithfulness. My mother lost it. She suggested counseling, but to no avail. My father left us. This set the stage for the whole family to slowly spiral downward into the negative emotions that come from divorce.

Speaking for myself, deep down in my heart I thought it was because of me. But blaming myself just brought forth additional anger toward my father. As time went on, my anger grew—grew to the point that my mother could not handle me. My grades were affected as well as my whole being. I became rebellious. I would not listen or help around the house. I started hitting walls, doors, and windows. I was in the pits. Unable to cope, my mother now made a decision that would affect the rest of my life and send me deeper into the pit. For all weekends, holidays, and summers, she decided to send me to the ghetto of the South End of Boston to live with my aunt, where further abuse drove me into drugs and gang life.

Within every culture, there are a variety of families. As mentioned, these can range from drugs and alcohol to gangs and groups. Outside of drugs and alcohol, in my experience being accepted in a gang or group was another way of finding family. After coming home from boot camp, having done well, I had to further my training in California. It seems as if even in the Marine Corps there were little gangs. These gangs could range from five to ten people. I gravitated to one of these and became a leader. We were heavy drinkers, druggers, and fighters. My violent ways and impulsive, poor decisions kept people intimidated and at bay.

After my extended training, I came home and was "adopted" by the Kinkaid Park gang. There was no difference in behavior—it was still the heavy drinkers, druggers, and fighters. All of us had reputations. During my gang membership, I was able to sell drugs to support my habit, and I had a host of customers. As a gang member, I experienced acceptance and power, but my addiction soon led me to "go rogue." As a junkie, the gang family could not fill the void, only the drugs. Toward the end I wandered rogue from one city to another, from one bar to another, and as time went on every bar, even biker bars came to exclude and avoid me. Rejection, however, never left. At the end, I was filled with loneliness, searching but never finding a family.

Such anger I held and nurtured because of my broken family. I told my mother one time I would kill my father—what hate! The hard thing to understand was that I blamed myself for the failure of my family, but that hurt too much, so I needed to blame someone else. The someone else was my father. Writing this brings to me a spirit of peace—it is as if a demon was just released. I understand now. I can say that the root of a great deal of my anger stemmed from the hate I had for my dad. What a cancer, Jesus—forgive me for my hate, and I pray that you take this and replace it with love and mercy.

Coming from a broken family gives one a sense of disconnection. For much of my life before Christ, this disconnection led me to try connecting to something other than God. After the demise of my original family, I chose to be connected to the family of drugs, alcohol, and groups of people who had common interests. The drugs accepted me, as well as the groups (until I went rogue). My feelings at that time were, "It is better to be accepted by these than wander in life with desperate loneliness." But still deep in my heart the seed of God was planted. Let no one say that the word of the Lord does not reach people. Sometimes a seed takes longer to open; therefore the fruit takes longer to grow. The drugs and alcohol were a barrier or rock, so to speak, that covered the seed of truth that was planted. This barrier or rock was strong, but not stronger than the word of God, which gave a choice, a choice of adoption into *His* family. As the barrier or rock was broken, the seed sprouted up from His Son Jesus and the word. With this came the choice of truth that sets free, and this truth would make its way to the surface when the time was right.

For the longest period of time I lived alone—my heart, me, and my drugs—Mr. Tough Guy. When I accepted Christ, I realized how much I was a frightened boy using whatever means to stuff down the feelings. Another thing I realized was that I had an obsession to die. Christ gave me purpose, a purpose to live and go forward.

I became a new person and joined another gang, so to speak, the gang or family or body of Christ, who combat fear and intimidation with love and hope. I am not going to say today, twenty-eight years later, that it has all been a day at the beach. But what I *can* say is I would rather live in the embrace of the Lord, eternally, than be a part of a worldly gang that transfers their own fear to others through intimidation and violence. Father, forgive me for all the people I have harmed. Broken because of your love, I no longer have to live with or be accepted in a gang.

Heirs with Christ

So then, brothers, we are debtors, not to the flesh, to live according to the flesh. For if you live according to the flesh you will die, but if by the Spirit you put to death the deeds of the body, you will live. For all who are led by the Spirit of God are sons of God.

> For you did not receive the spirit of slavery to fall back into fear, but you have received the Spirit of adoption as sons, by whom we cry, "Abba! Father!" The Spirit himself bears witness with our spirit that we are children of God, and if children, then heirs—heirs of God and fellow heirs with Christ, provided we suffer with him in order that we may also be glorified with him. (Rom. 8:12–17)

For many years I have had to struggle with the decision my parents made regarding the family and me. But I have been able to rise above it, empowered by Jesus through the Holy Spirit in dealing with my parents' divorce. Today divorce is on the rise, and who better to help children who are a product of this terrible problem than someone like me who experienced God's healing from the fallout of divorce and empowerment from this. Working with youth over the last twenty-four years, I have been enabled to share oneness in Christ, bringing healing to children, youth, and young adults who are experiencing the fallout of divorce.

What a blessing it has been to connect with these youth. Looking in retrospect, I would not change a thing regarding my parents' divorce! As painful as it was, God has changed the brokenness from my family into the oneness of a deeper relationship with Jesus, healing me even as I reached out to serve the Body of Christ.

Resources to Contact for Help

Disclaimer: Not all resources listed are necessarily Christian, nor can I vouch for their quality or contact info. Do your own research before contacting, but be safe in using a computer—search information cannot always be erased.

Call 9-1-1 if you are in immediate danger.

Our greatest need is a relationship with Jesus! Call 1-888-NEEDHIM (633-3446)

Online lists of many types of hotlines: keepthefaith.com/page/crisis-help, yourcross.org/hotlines

Focus on the Family: 1-800-AFAMILY (232-6459) or 1-855-771-HELP, focusonthefamily.com

Family Life: 1-800-FL-TODAY (358-6329), familylife.com

Billy Graham Association: 1-877-772-4559, billygraham.org

Grace Help Line 24 Hour Christian service 1-800-982-8032

The 700 Club Hotline 1-800-759-0700

13

Brokenness from Abandonment

Into Oneness through Tough Love

THE YEAR WAS 1972, and I was thirteen. Going downstairs in our basement, I searched for some bamboo poles. Our basement was not finished and had a steep stairway going down from the kitchen. The walls were made of granite and had white paint that was chipping off. You could see the floor joists exposed in the ceiling. Hanging from them were the heating pipes wrapped in asbestos. The basement was warm with all these heating pipes originating there, ascending up to the radiators on the other floors. In the floor joists were cavities where items were stored. Searching in them, I found the bamboo poles. Along with this, I found a variety of sharp knives. Searching further, I was able to locate some twine. Using these items, I made a series of weapons. My intention was to use these weapons to kill my father.

The day was always long at school. On this day it was even longer. The school I attended was Sterling Junior High, located a fair distance from my house. In the mornings I would rise to either to walk or catch the bus, which in most cases I missed. The school was old, and each floor was lined with dark-green lockers. The walls were painted in light brown and institutional green. The floors were vinyl with a dirty brown color. The hallways seemed long, and if you gave a good holler, you would hear an echo. On the bottom floor was the cafeteria. This was the venue for me to start expressing my anger toward my parents' divorce and my feelings of abandonment.

The cafeteria was a place where cliques of various types of students could be easily spotted. This day, when the lunch bell rang, I chose to pick a fight with one of the "toughies." Going to class after the bell, I noticed that this boy had pointed shoes. They were black leather, and this was what the toughies wore. I decided to tease the boy about his shoes. Doing this caused hostilities between him and me, to put it mildly. This set the stage for a brutal fight after school.

The end-of-the-day bell rang, and I was feeling anxious about the fight I was going to have. We met down the hill behind the school, where I whipped this kid and his friend as well. After the fight was over, I went home to a scolding from my mother. My father no longer lived with us, so I didn't have to worry about him. After a series of these scuffles, and continued defiance toward my mother, she decided to send me to her brother's house in Boston's South End ghetto. Every weekend, holiday, and summer off from school, my mother would send me on my way. Send me away like a broken toy that no one wanted anything to do with. Abandoned by my parents, broken, angry, rejected, and confused, I now had to endure life with compounded abuse at my relatives' house.

In the divorce of my parents, I experienced abandonment. But this started earlier, even before the divorce. The divorce just exacerbated the feeling. When I was molested was when I first felt abandoned, because nothing was done about the abuse. The second time I felt abandoned was when my parents discarded and sent me to Boston, the pit of abuse. Abandonment and being discarded set the stage for a feeling I would have to endure for a long time, even as a born-again Christian. Questions that haunted me were, "Why? Aren't I worthy to be a son?"

Abandonment is the trigger to many feelings I have had to deal with. The one that most bothered me was *rejection*. It still does! And rejection would trigger anger and rage. During the time I was not a Christian, I would act on these emotions by harming people. After accepting the Lord, I had to learn how not to. This was not easy. Not acting on these emotions by harming others, I learned to implode, stuffing them down inside myself. This would cause me to get depressed. With all this happening, one might ask how God could use this to bring me into oneness with Him for His glory.

My experience being abandoned made me avoid getting close to anyone. I did not want to take a chance on it happening again! This caused me to isolate by using the tools of the world, meaning drugs, sex, money, etc. These kept me from connecting first with God and secondly with others. So I wandered bewildered and alone, never dealing with my past and these chains that bound me. God had to break me free from these. In the end, God needed to use tough love to keep me from wallowing in a pity-party singing "poor, poor pitiful me," so afraid of rejection that I would act in ways to keep others from ever getting close to me.

The haunting questions "Why?" and "Aren't I worthy to be a son?" became an instrument of Satan to draw me into deep depression from any kind of rejection. However, as I matured, rejection by many people and groups would become another kind of instrument. Abandonment and rejection actually became the tough love instrument *God* used to teach me maturity in Him, and therefore bring closure and freedom and peace in *Him*, and not people.

Let me explain. The last word in the previous paragraph is *people*; I mention this because I became a people pleaser. People-pleasing became a vile tool I used to deal with abandonment. If I pleased people, I would be accepted by them, and therefore would be able to deal with my deep-rooted abandonment/rejection issues. This was purely in vain!

The habit would become a vicious cycle and was extremely selfish. I would just find myself depressed whenever I felt rejected again. God finally got through to me and helped me truly understand this only when I was rejected by a mission field! This happened when I was the volunteer youth director at Springhill Presbyterian. Let me tell you the story.

I worked hard with the youth to raise money. The church was excited about the mission trip. The cause was a noble one. Through a series of events, I revealed that I had HIV to a pastor who was going on the trip. He was far from gracious. In a low moment, he judged me and said I needed to tell the mission field organization. I obliged, only to be told they did not want me there because I might bleed on somebody![1] Abandonment! Rejection! Wow! Did this hit me hard! But what hit me harder was God's grace! What I mean is that after I struggled for a time with this rejection even by God's people, God told me to tell the youth to take the money we raised and go on the trip without me. He told me also the Scripture verses below.

> And Jesus said, "Father, forgive them, for they know not what they do." (Luke 23:34)

> Blessed are the peacemakers, for they shall be called sons of God. (Matt. 5:9)

---

[1] Incidentally, I *was* injured and bled on another mission trip, and nobody got HIV! (I *did* insist they use gloves in treating me.)

Putting into practice the word of God is the hardest thing I have had to do; however, it is also the greatest!

So in a low moment I found a high moment and moved forward in maturity. If I had caused a commotion regarding the "violation of my rights" so to speak and brought this to the attention of the courts, many people would not have experienced the grace of God on this mission field. As I am loved by Christ, through Him I am able to emulate His love to others in my low moments. In this low moment of rejection, God helped me come to a degree of closure with abandonment and rejection—what a paradox! How interesting that the pinnacle of our salvation occurred when Jesus took our sin in His body on the cross and cried out, "My God, my God, why have you forsaken me?" Our Savior understands when we feel abandoned! He also has felt that, to a far greater degree than we ever can, when our sins separated Him from any sense of the Father's presence. We are most like Christ when He allows us to be rejected even as we are attempting to love others in His name!

Of course I am not the only one in the world that has felt abandoned. In my volunteering, and working as a professional social worker, I have been able to see the fallout. God used my experience of abandonment to mold me—mold me in a way that took from me my contempt for my parents, and gave me understanding of what one goes through in abandonment. I do not want to over-generalize my experience for others, but what God was doing in me was making a way to connect and minister to others who feel abandoned or rejected.

This brokenness brought to fruition, once again, a deeper oneness with God. God's tool in helping me deal with abandonment was the tough love of rejection, rejection from institutions that I involved myself with, both secular and religious. *This rejection* made me feel brokenness. It helped me understand and have empathy for others who experience abandonment and rejection. It reminded me that my self-worth comes not from the approval or acceptance by others but from the love of God seen in Jesus on the cross, the love that says, "I will never leave you nor forsake you!"[2] It put me in the privileged position of emulating my Lord by suffering for others. And it empowered and taught me how to love and help youth and others who have been abandoned or rejected. Praise be to God for His tough love!

Resources to Contact for Help

> Disclaimer: Not all resources listed are necessarily Christian, nor can I vouch for their quality or contact info. Do your own research before contacting, but be safe in using a computer—search information cannot always be erased.
>
> Call 9-1-1 if you are in immediate danger.

---

[2] See Deuteronomy 31:6 and Hebrews 13:5.

Our greatest need is a relationship with Jesus! Call 1-888-NEEDHIM (633-3446)

Nine-Line Nationwide crisis/suicide: 1-800-999-9999 (For runaways and homeless youth, and their families. Provides short term counseling over the phone.)

Online lists of many types of hotlines: keepthefaith.com/page/crisis-help, yourcross.org/hotlines

Focus on the Family: 1-800-AFAMILY (232-6459) or 1-855-771-HELP, focusonthefamily.com

Billy Graham Association: 1-877-772-4559, billygraham.org

Grace Help Line 24 Hour Christian service 1-800-982-8032

The 700 Club Hotline 1-800-759-0700

14

Brokenness from Addiction

Into Oneness through Acceptance

WEBSTER DEFINES ADDICTION as the quality or state of being addicted or being an addict. An addict is defined as one who has devoted or surrendered oneself to something habitually or obsessively. So addiction is the condition of being devoted or surrendered or even a slave to a habit or obsession. Often addiction is used more narrowly to refer to a compulsive physiological or psychological need for a habit-forming drug. Certainly in my life that was the case! But it is not just drugs and alcohol that are addicting. People can be addicted to gambling, eating, shopping, work, video games, body building, wealth, fame, power, pornography, sex, and especially *self*—just about anything! Take a look in the mirror! What might *you* be addicted to? What controls *your* life?

Starting with the breakup of my family, you have seen how drug addiction was a constant context and problem throughout much of my life. The first substance I abused was alcohol. I remember my father on his day off getting up in the morning and drinking a shot of whisky, followed by a beer. I was five or six years old. Once he asked me if I wanted a taste of his beer, which I accepted. I enjoyed the tingling fizzle and also the taste. My father continued to offer me tastes, and eventually I began to sneak beer out of the refrigerator for myself, afraid of getting whipped for stealing his beer. I didn't drink enough to get intoxicated, I just liked the taste.

Then one evening, when I was eleven and visiting my cousins in Virginia, they offered me a beer, which led to drinking many more, and I got drunk. This was far from the innocent experiences I had in Virginia catching fireflies and swimming in the river. I remember spinning around in a dizzying daze followed by puking in the toilet.

Later at my aunt's house in Boston's South End, I had access to a whole host of drugs. When my cousins went downstairs, they often left roaches (marijuana cigarettes) burning in the ashtrays. Once when they left, I picked one up and started smoking it. My cousin came back upstairs and caught me. He asked me if I wanted to get high. I said, "Yes!" He pulled out a small brown envelope with about ten dollars worth of pot in it and rolled a joint for us to smoke. I caught an enormous buzz and got wasted for the first time.

Reeling from my parents' divorce, my abuse, and being abandoned, I began to use various drugs (marijuana, downers, uppers, methamphetamine, acid, and cocaine) to make it through each day, as I mentioned in chapter 2. Marijuana and downers would suppress my feelings of worthlessness and help me sleep. Uppers and methamphetamine would suppress my feelings of hunger and help me work the long twelve- and fourteen-hour days. Acid was a recreational drug, which I would take when relaxing. By age seventeen I was a full-blown drug addict, and was also addicted to pornography. These addictions ravaged my life and are a temptation and potential threat even to this day! (For an example of what they did to a young woman I was friends with, see chapter 15.) Seeing the damage they have done, and the multiple other problems they have caused for me and others, I wish so much that I had never been introduced or given in to them. The message so prevalent today that such things are okay is a lie from the pit of hell! In reality they were masters that enslaved me. What I didn't realize at the time is that they were false and destructive *substitutes* for the one true and loving Master I was *created* to serve.

> [Jesus said,] "No one can serve two masters, for either he will hate the one and love the other, or he will be devoted to the one and despise the other. You cannot serve God and money." (Matt. 6:24)

The Bible does not use the word *addiction*. But it does talk about the things that function as masters in our lives. In Matthew 6, Jesus says, "No one can serve two masters; for either he will hate the one and love the other, or he will be devoted to the one and despise the other. You cannot serve God and mammon [wealth]."[1] The earliest Christian statement of faith was "Jesus is Lord." *Lord* is another word for *master*. In the very first of the Ten Commandments, God says, "I am the Lord your God...you shall have no other gods before me."[2] We were created to love and serve God as our *only* Master. But Satan tempts us to substitute many other things in place of God.

In my own life, these addictions or masters were habitual sins in which I used people, places, and things to fill the void or take the place of God in my life. In 1 Corinthians 6, the Apostle Paul writes about these addictions or masters that take the place of God in so many lives. He writes, "Do you not know that the unrighteous will not inherit the kingdom of God? Do not be deceived; neither the sexually immoral, nor idolaters, nor adulterers, nor sexual perverts, nor thieves, nor the greedy, nor drunkards, nor revilers, nor robbers will inherit the kingdom of God." Wow, that sounds like the person I was before accepting Christ! Paul goes on: "And such were some of *you*. But *you* were washed, *you* were sanctified, *you* were justified in the name of the

---

[1] Matthew 6:24
[2] Exodus 20:2–3

Lord Jesus Christ and in the Spirit of our God" (emphasis added). That sentence was written to *me!* (Notice also that it says "such *were* some of you"! These people were *delivered* from their addictions through their relationship with Jesus Christ!) After these examples of addictions or masters comes one of the clearest descriptions of addiction in the Bible: "'All things are lawful for me,' but not all things are *helpful.* 'All things are lawful for me,' but I will not be enslaved [mastered] by anything" (emphasis added).[3] Addiction is not restricted to drugs, porn, gambling, or just the better known addictions—it applies to *anything* that enslaves or masters us, that *takes the place of God* in our lives or hinders our relationship with Him.

> "All things are lawful for me," but not all things are helpful. "All things are lawful for me," but I will not be enslaved by anything. (1 Cor. 6:12)

Mankind has been struggling with addiction or substitute masters since the very beginning. In the Garden of Eden, Satan tempted Eve and Adam with the sin of being their own masters, and they fell for it![4] We have been suffering the consequences ever since. In the fourth chapter of Genesis, we learn about Adam and Eve's sons, Cain and Abel, and how sin became a master in the heart

---

[3]   1 Corinthians 6:9–12, RSV
[4]   See Genesis 3

of Cain. Both Cain and Abel brought an offering to the Lord, a sacrifice to be burned on an altar. Since Cain grew crops, he brought some of those. Since Abel tended sheep, he brought some of those. The Bible says the Lord had regard, or approval, for Abel's offering, but not for Cain's. We aren't told why the Lord rejected Cain's offering. The New Testament comments that Cain's deeds were evil, and he was not motivated by faith.[5] Perhaps his sacrifice was not accepted because his heart attitude was not right, as implied by these comments, and as we can see in the incident that follows. In any case, Cain becomes angry when his offering is rejected. Then the Lord says to him, "Why are you angry, and why has your countenance fallen? If you do well, will you not be accepted? And if you do not do well, sin is couching [waiting in ambush] at the door; its desire is for you, but you must master it." But Cain did not heed the Lord's instruction. He allowed his jealousy, his sin, to master *him* and ended up killing his brother Abel.[6] By the sixth chapter of Genesis, sin has mastered almost all of mankind, and God sends judgment by flooding the world, saving only godly Noah and his family.

God tells Cain he must master the sin waiting to ambush him. But the only way to do that is by letting God take His rightful place as Master (Lord) in our life. Only God is a loving Master. Only He has the power to overcome sin's

---

[5]   See 1 John 3:12 and Hebrews 11:4

[6]   Genesis 4:3–8

mastery. When we invite Him in by accepting Jesus as Lord and Master, He fills us with the Holy Spirit who gives us the power to overcome sin and all other addictions. But we must allow Him to be Lord over every part of our lives if we want to be delivered from the things that enslave us.

The two big deceptions in my life were first, that things of the world could or would fill the void in my life meant to be filled by God, and second, that I could master my addictions on my own. Before I was a Christian, it was easy for me to be a drug addict, glutton, or just plain addicted to anything that would make me happy for the moment. When I became a Christian, I realized the only Master I need is Jesus. But even after becoming a Christian, I fell prey to the deception that I could master my addictions on my own. Only Jesus has the power to defeat these addictions, and only by depending on Him can I be delivered from them.

The Apostle Paul wrote about this struggle with sin in his letter to the Romans. He did not understand his own actions. He said the good he *wanted* to do he did *not* do, and the evil he did *not* want to do he *did!* Who could deliver him from this struggle? Only God, through Christ Jesus our Lord![7] How many times we don't understand our own actions, wondering why we keep doing the things we know are wrong! Only Christ can deliver us from this vicious cycle of sin!

---

[7]   Romans 7:15–25

Kinds of Addictions

(Note: support groups listed below as examples are not necessarily endorsed by the authors; a list of support group ministries and organizations with their phone numbers and websites can be found at the end of this chapter)

Before we can begin to deal with our various addictions, we must first recognize what they are! In the following paragraphs, I list some of the more common ones as an aid to help you discover what yours might be. Among these are the classical "seven deadly sins." Addictions can be divided into different categories. Some are obvious bad addictions recognized by society and having their own support groups. Others are not as obvious and could be described as too much of a good thing. Then there is a final spiritually deep addiction I would describe as the essence of evil! The National Association for Christian Recovery (nacr. org) lists and provides links to both Christian and secular organizations for support groups for many of the types of addiction listed below.

Substance abuse, especially of *illegal drugs* and *prescription pain killers*, is the first thing people think of when we talk about obviously bad addictions. This is the one that has done the most damage in my life. No amount of cocaine or heroin is good for you! Taking acid or sniffing glue is just stupid! So are many other substances people experiment with today. (See chapter 16 for a description of a day in the life of a junkie.) But this category also includes *alcohol*, which is accepted by society but causes a far higher percentage of problems in terms of drunk driving fatalities, ruined families, and destroyed lives than the illegal drugs do, overall. (This is not a suggestion to legalize drugs—that would just increase the problem!) Certainly *smoking and nicotine* fall in this category also, as one of the most addictive substances known to man, which has caused many deaths and health problems. *Legal drugs or medicines* can lead to addiction, especially those used for pain. Just because a doctor prescribes it doesn't mean it can't be a problem for you (and such prescriptions have led to an explosion in opioid and heroin addiction and overdose deaths in recent years). And even *caffeine* can be a problem when it is used excessively. Groups such as Alcoholics Anonymous (AA) and Narcotics Anonymous (NA) and the Christian program Celebrate Recovery (CR) attempt to help addicts recover and stay sober. Al-Anon is a group that helps family members of alcoholics. The National Association for Christian Recovery (NACR) has a list of ministries and group organizations for many types of addictions.

Pornography (the deadly sin of lust) and **sexual addictions** are other obviously bad addictions, and they are widespread among men but increasingly affect women also. There are many variations of these addictions, some rejected by society (such as child porn and pedophilia) and some accepted (like strip clubs and adult bookstores). But Christians and others who accept God's value system understand that pornography leads to the objectification of persons and also comparison of remembered images with current relationships, and it can easily become a master in our lives that destroys those relationships. The Internet, with its privacy and ease of access, has enabled many to be tempted and overcome by this addiction. There are many other sexual addictions also. Pornography has damaged my view of women, and only Christ has helped me overcome this addiction. Prodigals International, Focus on the Family, and FamilyLife all provide resources for helping deal with pornography and sexual addictions.

Gambling is an addiction that has multiplied greatly in our society since the arrival of state lotteries. Often it is a "lucky" winning streak that convinces someone that they can beat the system and that even heavy losses can be recovered when their "luck returns." Gamblers Anonymous tries to help people break this habit that can also ruin lives and relationships.

Materialism or the addiction to money or possessions (the deadly sin of greed) is a subtle but pervasive danger in our affluent society, but even those less fortunate can fall victim to this obsession with things and having *more*. Jesus said, "Take care, and be on your guard against all covetousness, for one's life does not consist in the abundance of his possessions."[8] God

---

[8]   Luke 12:15; see also Matthew 6:24–33

knows we need various things, but when desire or obsession with those things, or with always having *more* of them, begins to be a master in our lives, we need God's help to overcome them. There may be support groups somewhere for this, but I think one of the best antidotes is to go on a mission trip to an impoverished country! Recently international evangelist and Ugandan church planter Pastor Richard Nyakaana stayed with us for a few months. He oversees six churches, supports forty-five orphans, and leads evangelistic rallies in Uganda, as well as doing revival preaching in America. His family doesn't own a refrigerator, let alone a microwave!

Vanity or addiction to <u>recognition</u> or <u>fame</u> is something we expect to see in Hollywood or among celebrities, but in a society focused on appearances, it can become a controlling influence among all of us "little people" as well. Notice how many advertisements are for products that make us look better, or seem cooler, or hotter. (How did those words become synonyms anyway?) Some eating disorders, such as anorexia and bulimia, are not really about food but rather about control and appearances, not wanting to appear "fat." Some people even commit crimes to gain public notoriety. Although the world may focus on appearance, the Bible says *God* looks at our *heart*.[9] Meditating on the character and works of God/Jesus/Spirit, studying His word, and participating in praise and worship are some of the things

---

[9] I Samuel 16:7

that can help us be more humble about our own little part in God's eternal plan!

Power trips or an obsession with control is an addiction not limited to politicians and dictators. The term "control freak" applies to many who feel a need to completely control all or some aspects of their or others' lives. Often this is motivated by fear that is the result of something in our lives that has been "out of control." I have pointed out the "illusion of control" I tried to maintain by building business empires, attempting to compensate for the abuse and addictions I could not control earlier in my life. The failures, disasters, and suffering that come along in any life will eventually pierce this illusion of control, but only total surrender to Jesus as Lord can solve it. Parenting a two-year-old or having a cat can also help.

Violence (the deadly sin of wrath) is often a result of anger issues or rage that comes from frustration over things that are beyond one's control. My own rage at my father for his abuse and abandonment of me and of my mother led to acts of violence against others and myself. At times I could easily have killed someone else, or myself. Jesus told us the commandment against murder applies equally to the heart attitude of anger or putting others down.[10] Anger is almost always a secondary emotion, so it will help to figure out what primary emotion is prompting it and why. Violence and

---

[10] Matthew 5:21–22

anger are often increased through entertainment choices and video games that rehearse violent thoughts and justify that type of thinking. And alcohol or drugs combined with anger can get us quickly out of control. The general solution for this addiction is to try to understand why we are angry and who our anger is really about. Then put ourselves in the other person's shoes and understand what it is like to be them. Then seek reconciliation and peace.[11] It was not until I realized my father had never received "the blessing" from *his* father that my heart began to soften. Contemplating the suffering Jesus went through in order to save us, because of His great love for us while we were still sinners, will help us see the need for us to pass along His forgiveness. If video games or entertainment choices or alcohol are tempting or causing us to sin in this area, we need to cut them out of our life.[12] General or anger management counseling may also help. The National Anger Management Association has lists of specialists.

The above addictions are ones that seem obviously *bad*. But there are many addictions that involve *good* things that are blessings from God or are necessary for life. In these cases, the problem is "too much of a good thing" that interferes with God's purposes in our lives. Here again, Jesus's general command is to cut out of our lives anything

---

[11] See Matthew 5:21–26
[12] See Matthew 5:30

that is causing us to sin.[13] If we can cut something back to the point where it is *not* causing us to sin, then maybe that is okay. Even then, we must prayerfully consider whether an activity is consistent with our faith, for as the Bible says in Romans 14:23, "Whatever does not proceed from faith is sin." For many of these categories, meeting with a pastor or Christian counselor may be helpful.

Video games are not inherently evil (except for ones that have sexually explicit or excessively violent content). They can help children learn things, develop eye-hand coordination, and have healthy competition with friends. But they can also be very addicting. The word *addicting* is even used as a "positive" feature in advertisements for many games! Yet such addictions have destroyed marriages and lives. My friend Charlie Winkelman encouraged me to write about his addiction to a particular video game named Civilization. It was easy for him to justify the need to relax after a long day at work. That would have been fine if it was only an hour or two, but it began to cause him to stay up late and lose sleep, negatively impacting other parts of his life. Soon it became apparent to me it was going to really hurt his relationships and ability to minister to others. I confronted him about this over a long period of time, and finally a spiritual moment on a mission trip convinced him of his addiction and need to give it up. Setting a time limit for ourselves or young people is a good first step here.

---

[13]   Matthew 5:30

Entertainment addictions occur when a particular type of entertainment, which can be a blessing in and of itself (e.g. music, sports, television, movies, board and card games, etc.) begin to take over an increasing amount of time or resources, and as a result negatively impact other life responsibilities and even our relationship with God. (Addictions to things like *e-mail* and *Facebook* are similar to this category.) In my own life, I enjoyed watching the Boston Celtics on TV. There's nothing wrong with that in itself, but it began to function as an escape to take me away from the pain in my life and the void from not having a deep relationship with God through Jesus Christ. I still like the Celtics, but they no longer draw me away from God.

Shopping is an addiction for many people, who find self-esteem through buying things. This is sometimes but not always related to the addiction called **hoarding,** which involves an inability to let go of stuff. These addictions can affect finances and relationships negatively, as well as be a substitute for a relationship with God.

Food addictions (the deadly sin of gluttony) are particularly difficult to deal with because we all need food! We can't "just say no" and give it up! The problem comes when we confuse needs with wants. Right before I came to Christ, I weighed 370 pounds. My friend Danny and I would order literally hundreds of dollars of food from the local Chinese restaurant for a single meal! We loved to eat! At the end of an hour-long eat-a-thon, we would be lying down rubbing our distended bellies and passing out in front of the TV. To this day, I struggle with portion control, although healthier choices and eliminating gorging episodes have enabled me to get down to 255! There are many organizations that can help with this addiction (e.g., Weight Watchers, Jenny Craig, Nutrisystem, Overeaters Anonymous). Diet pills and diets usually don't help. Changing your lifestyle to eat less and exercise more is necessary. The opposite problem of eating disorders, such as anorexia or bulimia, is more about control and self-image and having their own support groups and hotlines (e.g., National Eating Disorders Association). Surrendering this whole area of life to God's guidance is crucial.

Workaholism is an addiction that didn't grab a hold on me until *after* I came to Christ and was drug-free enough to work! Each time I built one of my three electrical-construction company empires I became excessive, working sixteen- to eighteen-hour days, seven days a week. Excellence is a godly goal in our work, for Scripture calls us to "work as unto the Lord,"[14] but this can easily slip over into the additional addiction of **perfectionism**. For example, I would hire men to do particular jobs, and they did okay, but I wanted better and would redo their work myself! Compared with drugs, work is a more productive enterprise, but it can also become an idol, stroking our pride

---

[14] Colossians 3:23

and taking us away from family, relationships, ministry, and other God-given responsibilities. Eventually I learned that my time is a valuable gift I have been given, and I need to manage it in a balanced way according to God's priorities, making sure He is part of every moment. Our work is important to God, providing resources as well as opportunities for witness, but only my work for *God*, under *His* direction and power, will make a difference for eternity.

Hobbies were not an area I struggled with, but for many people, these activities can consume their attention and leave little time for God's priorities, especially relationships. Again, balance and God's guidance through His Spirit and word are the key to not letting a hobby become a master or idol.

Exercise was a whole new world for me as I worked to maintain my sobriety. It started as I bought dumbbells to work out in the basement of the halfway house. These weights are appropriately named! Like many other endeavors in my life, I quickly became excessive. If others thought an hour or two a day was sufficient, I drove myself to work out four to five, with only two days a week off. After my various injuries, I thought working out could take the place of pain medication! This was not the case. The excessive workouts only furthered my injuries and exacerbated my problems with pain medication. The Apostle Paul says that bodily training is of some value, but training in godliness is far more important.[15] Today I find that forty minutes of bodily exercise a day is quite sufficient, and that the spiritual disciplines of Bible study and prayer pay even greater dividends.

Family is a good gift from God, perhaps His best gift besides salvation! It is His building block for human society, a model for His Church, and an illustration of the spiritual relationships that are the heart of God's plan for us (e.g. a Heavenly Father seeking His lost children, and Christ as a husband laying down His life for His bride—the Church). But like any of God's good gifts, even family can become an idol. The American dream of being successful includes having a loving family in a nice home. As I mentioned in chapter 5, this was a dream for me, a hope that contrasted with my own broken family. When I moved to Virginia, one of my dreams was to reconcile and rebuild my own broken family. I paid for holiday meals and gave expensive gifts, thinking this would put the family back together. But God's plan was different. He later *did* bring my family to a point of forgiveness and reconciliation, through the death of my mother, but not through my own earlier desperate attempts. As Charlie and I work with the After School Kids at church, we notice the grade school children, who are often from broken homes, talking about their boyfriends and girlfriends at an age much younger than usually associated with such

---

[15]   1 Timothy 4:8

relationships. They too are sensing the dream of family. Some young parents, vowing never to repeat the mistakes of *their* parents who were absent in some way, read books, listen to programs, and attend seminars (all good things in themselves) in an attempt to have "the perfect family." While family needs to be a higher priority for many, it must not take the place of *God*. Jesus affirmed family values and devotion, but He also said whoever loves father or mother or son or daughter more than Him is not worthy to be His disciple![16] Peter and the other disciples sacrificed time with their families to follow Jesus around the countryside for three years. The biblical patriarch Job, even after losing all of his children, still refused to curse God. In the movie *End of the Spear*, which tells the true story of five missionaries martyred while trying to bring the Gospel to a violent unreached tribe in South America, young Steve Saint asks his missionary father, "If the Waodani attack, will you defend yourself? Will you use your guns?" His father, Nate Saint, replies, "Son, we *can't* shoot the Waodani. They're not ready for heaven... we are." This father knew he had to follow Jesus, even if it meant losing his life and being unable to be there for his family. Those who make family an idol are unable to make that kind of sacrifice. However, no one should use this caution as an excuse to avoid fulfilling their God-given responsibilities to love, protect, nurture, and provide for their

---

[16]   Matthew 10:37

family, for the Bible reminds us, "If anyone does not provide for his relatives, and especially for his own family, he has disowned the faith and is worse than an unbeliever"!

Those are just some of the obviously bad and seemingly good addictions that people struggle with today. Any sin, or any activity or relationship, can become a master or idol in our lives. But there is a spiritually deep addiction that tempts *all* of us, a "master" that is the essence of evil, a sin by which the devil *became* the devil[17], and by which he then led the whole human race to their downfall—the addiction of self, or pride (the deadly sin of pride). **Pride** is the *ultimate* addiction, putting *self* above all other masters, and especially above our *true* Master, the Lord Jesus Christ. We fall naturally into this addiction—even as babies we are completely self-centered! We're born into sin, with a predisposition to addiction. This has been called original sin, the genetic legacy of Adam and Eve's fall from grace. Only people who have never parented a two-year-old disbelieve this! From the gang member displaying "machismo," to the biblical Pharisee believing himself better than other less pious people, to myself wanting this book to help others but worried how its success might tempt me, pride affects us all. Not just those who are vain or conceited, but even those with "low self-esteem" struggle with this addiction— they too are overly focused on "self"! We don't need higher

---

[17] See chapter on "The Great Sin" in C.S. Lewis' *Mere Christianity.*

"self"-esteem; we need higher "God" esteem! When we esteem God properly, we will see His love for us in the cross of Christ, and recognize our true worth in the price He paid. And pride is the one sin or addiction we must first surrender in order to accept Christ, who can help us overcome all other addictions! All of the various "Anonymous" twelve-step recovery groups (AA, NA, etc.) recognize the first step is admitting "I can't"—I can't beat this addiction without God's help. We must surrender our pride to accept the help God gives. Only the total surrender of our lives and all that we have to Jesus can defeat this ultimate addiction.

The Solution—Acceptance

The solution to the brokenness of addiction is acceptance. There are three things I must accept. First and foremost, I must accept that *I am addicted!* Born into sin and selfishness with a predisposition for addiction, I have fallen under the mastery of something other than God. All recovery group meetings start with an introduction in which you say who you are, and admit that you are an addict. Until we accept our addiction is real, we cannot make any progress in recovering from it.

Secondly, I must accept that *I have only one true Master, Jesus Christ,* who loved me and died for me so that I might have eternal life! The fourth-century church father, St. Augustine of Hippo, said, "Our hearts were made for you, O Lord, and they are restless until they rest in you." We were created by a loving God who desires a love relationship with us, but that has been broken by sins like addiction. Until I accept Christ as my Lord and Savior, I will not have the spiritual power to deal with my addiction, which has made something else the master of my life, taking His place.

And finally, I need to accept that *I need boundaries and accountability*, which God will help put in place in my life as practical means to aid my recovery. Boundaries are lines that I agree not to cross so that I won't be tempted by the addictive behavior. Accountability is regular contact with others who have agreed to help me maintain my boundaries. (Websites like nacr.org and CelebrateRecovery.com, which I *do* recommend, can help you find support groups and resources for help.) For example, because of the chronic pain I experience every day from my various past injuries, I have had a prescription for opioid-based medications. But because I am in recovery from past drug addiction, I experience temptation to take more of the medication than is prescribed, especially during the "manic" phase of my bipolar disorder. The boundary God helped me put in place was to have my friend Charlie control and dispense my medication on a regular basis, which also provided built-in accountability. Therefore the medication was able to serve me, rather than me serving it! (Quite recently, now in the spring of 2016, God led me to go through detox one more time to get off of this type of medication permanently, another step from brokenness toward oneness!)

The baggage of addiction doesn't usually vanish automatically when we become a Christian. There is still hard work to do in accepting our problem and God's solutions. But if we trust in Christ as our true Master, He will give us the help we need. The Apostle Paul affirmed this when he wrote, "No temptation has overtaken you that is not common to man. God is faithful, and He will not let you be tempted beyond your strength, but with the temptation will also provide the way of escape, that you may be able to endure it."[18] Often the "way of escape" involves help from pastors, counselors, support groups, books, and trusted friends that can help us face and recover from our addictions.

But now the ball is in *your* court! Denial that you have a problem *may* be the first indication that you indeed *have* a problem! Looking at your life, is there *anything* that comes between you and God, anything that you put *before* Him in any way?

Ask God to help you discern any other "masters" in your life. Then accept any problems revealed, accept Christ as your true Master and the *only* one who can help you deal with your problem, and accept the boundaries and accountability He helps you put in place—and you will experience greater Oneness with Him!

---

[18]   1 Corinthians 10:13

Resources to Contact for Help

Disclaimer: Not all resources listed are necessarily Christian, nor can I vouch for their quality or contact info. Do your own research before contacting, but be safe in using a computer—search information cannot always be erased.

Call 9-1-1 if you are in immediate danger.

<u>Christian organizations</u>

Our greatest need is a relationship with Jesus! Call 1-888-NEEDHIM (633-3446)

Online lists of many types of hotlines: keepthefaith.com/page/crisis-help, yourcross.org/hotlines

National Association for Christian Recovery: 1-888-551-NACR (6227), nacr.org (see "Finding a Support Group" under Referrals, lists many support groups for many types of addictions)

Celebrate Recovery (CR): celebraterecovery.com (Recovery groups in many churches)

Overcomers Outreach: 1-800-310-3001, overcomersoutreach.org (Christian group network)

Focus on the Family: 1-800-AFAMILY (232-6459) or 1-855-771-HELP, focusonthefamily.com

FamilyLife: 1-800-FL-TODAY (358-6329), familylife.com

Compass—Finances God's Way: 1-800-525-7000, compass1.org

Crown Financial Ministries: 1-800-722-1976, crown. org

Dave Ramsey solutions: daveramsey.com

Trinity Debt Management: 1-800-758-3844, trinity credit.org

Prodigals International: 1-866-910-9002, prodigal sinternational.org (sexual addictions, porn)

Billy Graham Association: 1-877-772-4559, billy graham.org

Grace Help Line 24 Hour Christian service 1-800-982-8032

The 700 Club Hotline 1-800-759-0700

Secular organizations

Alcoholics Anonymous (AA): 1-212-870-3400, aa.org (alcohol addiction groups)

Al Anon, Alateen: 1-757-563-1600, al-anon. alateen.org (for support of family members)

Dual Recovery Anonymous: draonline.org (both addiction and mental problems)

Gamblers Anonymous: 1-626-960-3500, gamblers anonymous.org (gambling addict. groups)

Narcotics Anonymous (NA): 1-818-773-9999, na.org (narcotics addiction groups)

National Anger Management Assoc: 1-646-485-5116, namass.org (anger mgmt. specialists)

National Institute of Diabetes & Digestive & Kidney Diseases: 1-301-496-3583, niddk.nih.gov (provides help in evaluating weight loss plans)

National Eating Disorders Association (NEDA): 1-800-931-2237, nationaleatingdisorders.org

15

Brokenness from Grief

Into Oneness through the Gospel

GRIEF OCCURS WHENEVER there is any kind of loss. The death of loved ones is especially difficult. As I have volunteered and worked in various communities over the years, I have experienced and seen the fallout of abuse, often with a tragic ending. I have seen many of my friends lose their quality of life because of abuse and drugs, then waste away and die of AIDS, outcast and alone. Their stories are heart-wrenching. Let me share one of them.

Lisa (not her real name) was a lovely, talented young woman with two wonderful children, who was a close dear friend of mine. Through Christ Jesus I survived *my* past—Lisa was not as fortunate. My hope is that she accepted Christ at her end and therefore is in heaven.

My dear friend was abused from a very young age, which led her into an abusive relationship with a man. Those who have never been abused find it hard to understand, but the fact remains that those who are abused as children often choose abusive spouses, perhaps because it is all they know, or even think they deserve. I remember consoling Lisa many times after her husband beat her. She told me how scared she was to do anything. Through a series of events, she broke up with her husband, only to experience the fallout of her being abused.

The sin of abuse led her to make choices that would destroy her life. She became a junkie as well as a prostitute. The period of time was 1980 to 1989. With the HIV/AIDS virus being spread among needle sharing groups, she contracted this disease in 1986. Because of this, she was ostracized by all her friends.

The year was 1990, and I was living at the three-quarter house[1] on Mount Ida Road in Dorchester, MA. During a phone call to my friend Danny, he informed me that Lisa had died. I was filled with sadness and a great sense of loss.

I wanted to share her story in my book with the hope that it would help others look at those who are abused not to judge them, but to know how the sin of abuse causes so

---

[1]   A house for graduates of the six-month program at a halfway house.

much damage and pain, and to gain compassion and love for the abused, and even for the abuser. This is what Jesus did for the woman at the well, the lepers, the blind, and all people. Jesus saw beyond the external characteristics. He saw the deeper things, things in the hollow of the heart, things I still had to learn.

Months prior to my friend's death, she asked me to do something. I did not understand it at the time, though I do now. It was my own shallowness out of ignorance, and the lack of seeing the heart, which kept me in my comfort zone and therefore I had no understanding. What she asked was so simple. She asked me to give her a hug. It was not until I became a Christian and was then challenged by the same conditions that I came to understand. Through Lisa's whole life, people had abused her because of the selfishness of sin, through gestures of either lust or anger, and she had truly never experienced a hug of genuine compassion and love! Sadly, many people experience the same tragic lack of true relationship, finding at the end of their lives only emptiness.

It was only a few months after my friend died that I was diagnosed with HIV.

Death is something that we all have to face. However, the sting of death no longer has its power when we are in Christ Jesus. Knowing people have accepted Christ takes away a great deal of the feelings of loss, so the mourning becomes less. Although this is the case, we still will cherish and miss the person who has died.

I have told you about my sense of loss from Lisa's death. I have not mentioned how I was able to deal with it. To be very candid, I am still having a hard time dealing with it.

I am having a hard time dealing with the death of many people in my life. This is because for many of them, I never knew if they had accepted the Lord and therefore have eternal life. What affects my feelings is that each person I knew that died had great qualities but was never able to put them to use, because of the disaster that comes from the brokenness of life, whether it was from abuse, a broken family, abandonment, death, disease, or extreme loss.

As I think of my friends, my heart breaks. Not because of my own self-centered loss, but because today I understand that they may never have believed and received Jesus and eternal life. So how have I been able to deal with death? I do *not* deal with it! I let *God* deal with it! How do I do this? By accepting that death is inevitable, and that we all have a choice either to rise above it by accepting the Lord and gaining His promised eternal life, or to evade the truth.

My friends both dead and alive, I could speculate, may not have escaped death, the death of the body or the death of still living. But God has promised me life in His Son, and I have chosen that life. For the longest time, I embraced death. I wanted to die, but for the wrong reasons. I wanted to die to escape the monsters that hung on me, the monsters of my past, and the monstrous feelings that were a product of abusive conditioning.

Death as seen by the world is an awful, tragic subject. However, it is different for people who have accepted Christ. We do not grieve as the world grieves, as the Bible says in 1 Thessalonians 4.

> But we do not want you to be uninformed, brothers, about those who are asleep, that you may not grieve as others do who have no hope. For since we believe that Jesus died and rose again, even so, through Jesus, God will bring with him those who have fallen asleep. For this we declare to you by a word from the Lord, that we who are alive, who are left until the coming of the Lord, will not precede those who have fallen asleep. For the Lord himself will descend from heaven with a cry of command, with the voice of an archangel, and with the sound of the trumpet of God. And the dead in Christ will rise first. Then we who are alive, who are left, will be caught up together with them in the clouds to meet the Lord in the air; and so we will always be with the Lord. Therefore comfort one another with these words. (1 Thess. 4:13–18)

Not that we are exempt from mourning for our loved ones who have died, but there is a celebration that follows for the one we have lost. This brings me to a question: How can the death of a loved one bring oneness with God? Let tell you some stories.

After my accident, as told in chapter 7, when I was crushed by a truck, I had moved in with my best friend Charlie. This was after he had just lost his dad, a devoted Christian and real "prayer warrior." As usual, one day, Charlie and I were in deep conversation, this one concerning the death of his dad. He expressed his deep feelings of loss. For a while I just listened. At that time I had not yet mourned the loss of a parent. But God spoke His words through me to tell Charlie that his father was now in heaven praying for us, much more effectively than before because He was with Jesus and could see our true needs more clearly now. I jokingly added that this was a really good thing since Charlie and I were now on the loose together! Charlie laughed and said he had never thought of it that way before. It was evident that the Holy Spirit led Charlie into oneness regarding his father's death and ascension to heaven. Charlie later told me my words had given him a lot of comfort.

Another way that death can lead to oneness is seen in the miracles that happened during my mother dying and after my mother's death (see chapter 9). A prayer that was always on my mother's heart was that her kids would be close as a family. This was always on my heart also. But given our various dysfunctions from our childhood experiences, this seemed nearly impossible. When I first moved to Virginia, I tried to pursue this, but with little success. I tried by investing in large meals during the holidays. My sister tried as well. We learned that holidays and food do not get to the heart of the problem. After each holiday meal, we would finish eating and go off into our own worlds and not talk about much. Year after year this was the case. Real "soul" food was missing. During my mother's death and after she died, there was a different kind of meal we experienced: the feast that Christ had for us, the feeding of our souls. What was offered at this meal was not turkey, ham, prime rib, etc., but the heavenly bread of Christ Himself and the cup of forgiveness and cleansing through His blood.

In the years leading up to my mother's death, Donna, Neal, and I never talked much about what had happened when we were children, and when we did, it was brief. Each one of us had resentment toward each other, and Mom and Dad as well. This all changed the evening following my mom's funeral, when we all sat down to commune both physically and spiritually. Sitting at the table, we all expressed how we felt, and Donna shared tearfully the joy and reconciliation she felt when Mom and she each asked and offered the other forgiveness. In the wake of her death, Mom's most fervent prayer in life was answered! That evening my mom sat in heaven with Jesus watching Donna, Neal, and I sit together as a family, sharing our feelings and our faith with each other, experiencing oneness as part of God's redeemed forever family!

> For God so loved the world, that he gave his only
> Son, that whoever believes in him should not perish
> but have eternal life. (John 3:16)

God said through the prophet Jeremiah, "I know the plans I have for you, plans for wholeness and not for evil, to give you a future and a hope."[2] Today I know God has a plan, a plan for me and others, now and forever. A plan to help people who experience the fallout of abuse, a plan to spread His word, a plan to love and plant love so that it may grow, and so that all will know that Jesus died to pay for our sins, but He rose again! This Good News or Gospel is the *only* answer to death and grief. Jesus ascended to heaven and sits on the right hand of the Father and advocates for us. So then, as we trust in Him, we will also escape death as Jesus did! This brings life, and the acceptance of death, in this world, and it brings life today and forever in Christ. So death for me has brought oneness with God, and in this oneness I have accepted death as a path to eternal life.

Resources to Contact for Help

> Disclaimer: Not all resources listed are necessarily
> Christian, nor can I vouch for their quality or contact
> info. Do your own research before contacting, but

---

[2]   Jer. 29:11

be safe in using a computer—search information cannot always be erased.

Call 9-1-1 if you are in immediate danger or feeling suicidal.

Our greatest need is a relationship with Jesus! Call 1-888-NEEDHIM (633-3446)

Online lists of many types of hotlines: keepthefaith. com/page/crisis-help, yourcross.org/hotlines

Focus on the Family: 1-800-AFAMILY (232-6459) or 1-855-771-HELP, focusonthefamily.com

Family Life Ministry: 1-800-FL-TODAY (358-6329), familylife.com

Billy Graham Association: 1-877-772-4559, billy graham.org

Grief Share groups: 1-800-395-5755, griefshare. org

Griefnet e-mail support groups: griefnet.org

Grace Help Line 24 Hour Christian service 1-800-982-8032

The 700 Club Hotline 1-800-759-0700

16

Brokenness from Disease

Into Oneness through Understanding

THE HISTORY OF the world both past and present has been plagued with disease, and virtually all have experienced this. But there is another disease that the world is plagued with; this is the disease of ignorance that comes from not knowing what is true as seen from the word of God and the Holy Spirit.

Diseases today are put in categories as described by doctors. Diseased *people* are also put in categories by many *other* people. As we go back in time, we see how people with a disease were treated. For example, in various times and places, those labeled as cripples, lepers, women that bled, those with the plague, the mentally ill, and persons having HIV/AIDS were put aside, ostracized and excluded from society.

One would think this is not case today, especially with all the knowledge that we have available. It is sad to say, however, that it still happens. People who have *been* diseased, or *are* diseased, still have to bear this burden, in many cases alone. In my experience of having hepatitis, syphilis, and HIV, it has been the abuse from others that has affected me more so than the physical ailments that accompanied the disease. When I was diagnosed in 1991, I was told I would only have two years left to live. This floored me. What floored me *more* was how my so-called friends *treated* me. Now that I was one of "them diseased, AIDS persons" I was pushed aside, ostracized, and excluded. I felt like a victim; however, I had a revelation from God. I am a victim only if I choose to be! I can rise above and choose another path. I attain to this by knowing Jesus and the truth that comes from the Holy Spirit, which leads to a far greater path, a path of selflessness. God has shown me that everyone can do the same through Jesus.

During the early eighties, among the news that swirled around us shooters was the report of a disease that was taking people down. They had named this gay cancer, ARC, and AIDS/HIV. There was little information, but it would not have mattered anyways. When you are sitting around with a ball of dope, the only thing in the atmosphere is getting the next fix.

Getting the next fix was easy as long as we had a supply of dope, but what was hard to get was a syringe. This being the case, sharing a needle was an ongoing practice. In many cases, there were four to eight people sharing one syringe.

Maintaining the syringe was a small job. We did not maintain the needle for cleanliness but more so to keep the needle sharp, because every entry into the flesh, hitting the vein, would dull the needle. Keeping the needle sharp would be done by sharpening the needle end on a match striker. It was 1980 when I first shot dope, and it was 1989 when I stopped. Let me give you a picture of a day in the life of a junkie.

The junkie rises from bed, in most cases feeling a bit sick. This starts the calling. In the back of the head, the monkey needs to be fed. At the time we all worked, and copping (finding drugs to buy on the street) was not hard. You had different types of junkies: coke-heads, speed-ballers, or just heroin users. It did not matter which one you were, you were still a junkie. All of us had a relationship with the needle. The needle was, in most cases, kept in a shoebox, along with cigarette filters, which were used as a dauber and filter so the pure part of the dope when drawn would go into the syringe. Also there was a silver spoon with the handle bent into itself.

If we had heroin, the first shot would bring a rush that gave an overwhelming feeling of contentment. If we were shooting coke, on entering the system it would give an unbelievable rush of elation, with ringing in the ears followed by a high sex urge.

Heroin would last six to eight hours, depending on the quality. This would keep a heroin addict from constantly shooting. However, a coke addict would have to chase the rush every twenty minutes until there was nothing left. This was followed by extreme depression and psychosis. The illusion that there is more coke somewhere is in the mind. In my experience as well what I saw with others, one finds oneself crawling on the floor and digging in shelves thinking one would find some.

In my and others' experience as heroin addicts, we would have some time of peace, only to succumb to the sickness that follows once the dope wears off. With the constant sharing of needles, you can imagine how much tainted blood was shared. But along with this, there was often sex added to the mix. I am not proud to say that my sex life was with many women. With this lifestyle, the chance of contracting HIV was high, and this would become a reality for me.

It was 1991, and I just had had a meeting with the director of the halfway house. Since I was high risk from needle sharing and the group of women I slept with, Dr. Bob Brown advised me to get tested. So I obliged him and set off the next day to Project Trust at Boston City Hospital. Entering the facility, I sensed a feeling of hollow, shallow darkness. What I mean is, no one spoke much of disease, but on the walls were posters that depicted this nightmare of the disease.

A counselor met me and briefed me regarding the procedures. He told me it would take two weeks before the results would come back. They took me in the back room where they drew five vials of blood from my veins. As they did this, the thought of "what if" mingled with my emotions. After drawing my blood, they gave me a follow-up appointment. The following two weeks were like walking with a concrete yoke around my neck.

It was the end of the two weeks. I awoke to a sunny morning. My appointment was early. Outside there was a brisk cold wind that drove through your skin. This was nothing compared to the chill I got when I was told I had HIV.

The HIV/AIDS disease was not well known. Institutions did not have a handle on the disease at this time, and many people were scared just saying the name. Throughout the country, people who had it were under persecution, even to the point of death. Many people were also dying a horrible death from the disease itself. This death was a product of the immune system's inability to fight off common everyday flues, colds, etc.

"Death Sentence" was the name for this disease among the people I knew who had it. After being told that I would not have long to live, I found myself in a whirlwind of emotions. I called Dr. Bob, and he told me to get back to the office soon. He quoted a Scripture from the Bible: Proverbs 3:5–8. "Trust in the Lord with all your heart and lean not on your own understanding; in all your ways acknowledge him, and he will make your paths straight. Do not be wise in your own eyes; fear the Lord and shun evil; this will bring health to your body and nourishment to your bones." I held this Scripture verse close to my heart, and it has come to life in my soul.

The next five years, I attended many support groups to find others to talk to. HIV brings feelings of being dirty and worthless. One feeling I had was, why bother with life? In the early 90s, you were given two years to live. Friends I knew were dying of AIDS and dying gruesomely. It started with catching another disease, followed by losing weight till you looked like a deflated human. Dwindling away, they soon died.

Seeing this, I pictured in my mind how I was going to die—would it be this gruesome death? Every day you wonder what disease you will die of and when. It is as if you had to accept that your time is next. Accompanying this was the stigma. Many people from all institutions were guilty of the stigma. We were rejected, misunderstood, and pushed aside. There were very few people you could openly talk to. There were a *few*. The hardest thing for me was the loneliness that accompanied my disease. On the other hand, God used this to change my perspective, and this He did in all areas of my life.

At one support group, I found a delightful worker to talk to as well as others who had the disease. This was at Neponset Health Center. The center had a meeting every Thursday evening for people surviving HIV/AIDS. The support group was great; however, over the years, faces disappeared and were replaced by tears. You could sense which ones were closest to death by the depleting of their bodies and their skeleton faces.

Death called for many, so they followed. This was hard, because in our minds we never knew who the reaper would call next. I attended for two years, and eventually stopped going. Too many people were dying; it was extremely sad.

Being diagnosed in 1991, I have had to live with this disease up till now. It is 2016, and I am still alive! I am overjoyed that medication has stopped the death toll from rising. But the miracle is that I have *never been on medication*! Not only did I not *die*, I have not had a *single health problem* from HIV! This is a miracle! One doctor recently couldn't believe it, so he had me retested to see if I really *had* HIV! I still tested positive, but with an extremely low viral load. One hundred thousand is considered high, while ten thousand is considered low. My load was eighty-four! Under eighty-two is undetectable! Furthermore, my T-cells have increased from five hundred to seven hundred, which outside of medication, according to my doctor, is impossible! My doctor was not a man of faith, so he wanted to study me to see what made me so different! Clearly, in this area of my life, God is truly at work, and the miracle worker Jesus is the cure for diseases and sin.

The biggest miracle, however, is how God has used this disease over the last twenty-five years to give me a wonderful new perspective, encompassing many areas. First, it changed the way I see others, especially relationships with women. Prior to me being diagnosed, my perspective of women was that they were for my own selfish desire, meaning selfish sexual gratification. During the first few years after being diagnosed, I went on many dates, and during these dates, I learned how to communicate by understanding the feelings and thinking of the women I dated.

Secondly, this disease was used to bring me perspective regarding rejection. As I have said, a major issue in my life was that my parents rejected me. In every case, once I told the women I dated that I had HIV, they rejected me. God used this to teach me how to deal with rejection. I have mentioned also the rejection I had to deal with from secular and religious institutions. What I learned was to understand what others were feeling. Jesus said on the cross, "Father, forgive them, for they do not know what they do." I learned to understand and have compassion for those who rejected me. Not that it came easy, but eventually forgiveness prevailed through the prompting of the Holy Spirit. This forgiveness that God gave me helped *me* to forgive people both past and present. This also happens daily in my walk with Christ.

If I should die from whatever, I truly know that this miracle came only through Christ as I've trusted in Him, and I have great anticipation of being raised to His glory. I end with this: if you have a disease, God may not take it away, but He will be waiting for you, not at your end, but at the beginning (of life eternal!), if you trust in Jesus. I have prayed for complete healing, but so far God has not done that.

2 Corinthians 12 (see below) explains His awesome purpose.

> So to keep me from being too elated by the surpassing greatness of the revelations, a thorn was given me in the flesh, a messenger of Satan to harass me, to keep me from being too elated. Three times I pleaded with the Lord about this, that it should leave me. But he said to me, "My grace is sufficient for you, for my power is made perfect in weakness." Therefore I will boast all the more gladly of my weaknesses, so that the power of Christ may rest upon me. For the sake of Christ, then, I am content with weaknesses, insults, hardships, persecutions, and calamities. For when I am weak, then I am strong. (2 Cor. 12:7–10)

When I asked God to take HIV/AIDS from me, He said this: "Eric, if I take this disease from you, but not from another, I will not be glorified; however, if I keep it in remission, then I will. Do not seek your own will, Eric, but seek my grace in this."

Resources to Contact for Help

Disclaimer: Not all resources listed are necessarily Christian, nor can I vouch for their quality or contact info. Do your own research before contacting, but be safe in using a computer—search information cannot always be erased.

Call 9-1-1 if you are in immediate danger.

Our greatest need is a relationship with Jesus! Call 1-888-NEEDHIM (633-3446)

Online lists of many types of hotlines: keepthefaith.com/page/crisis-help, yourcross.org/hotlines

Focus on the Family: 1-800-AFAMILY (232-6459) or 1-855-771-HELP, focusonthefamily.com

Family Life Ministry: 1-800-FL-TODAY (358-6329), familylife.com

Billy Graham Association: 1-877-772-4559, billy graham.org

Grace Help Line 24 Hour Christian service 1-800-982-8032

The 700 Club Hotline 1-800-759-0700

HIV/AIDS Initiative of Saddleback Church: 1-949-609-8000, hivaidsinitiative.com

American Cancer Society 1-800-227-2345

National Cancer institute 1-800-422-6237

Rest Ministries 1-888-751-REST (7378) (Chronic illness or pain)

17

Brokenness from Pain

Into Oneness through Focus on God

THE MORNINGS COME early. When they come, accompanying them is pain, pain that covers my whole body. As my eyes open, I slowly make my way out of bed to take medication, to stretch, take a hot shower, and work out. After doing these, the pain is lessened somewhat. But let me go back.

It was 1970, and our family was living in Quincy. That year the community was gathering to do a walkathon to raise money for people who had cancer. The walk was twenty-five miles. I was only eleven. This walk would be the beginning of pain. After walking sixteen miles, pain started radiating in my hip, causing me to limp. This incident led my parents to schedule an appointment with an orthopedic surgeon, Dr. Shiffman. Through a series of x-rays, I was diagnosed with slipped hips. I would have to undergo four surgeries, surgeries that put pins in me and then took them out over a period of four years. Eleven years old, and already my body was falling apart! But that was only the beginning.

It was 1996 when my company landed a job for the City of Boston's capital planning division, renovating the electrical system at a Dedham skating rink. At this job, I ruptured a cervical disk in my neck, causing a major hernia. I had to have emergency surgery then and additional surgery two years later.

Standing in front of my office in 2004 hiring a new hire, an employee in one of my trucks jumped the clutch sending the truck lunging forward, slamming me against the brick wall and breaking my pelvis. Somehow God used my body to push the truck off me. I fell to the ground trembling in shock, and in extreme pain.

My sister ran out asking if she should call an ambulance. In my shock, I told her no! I would be okay in a few minutes. Little did I know! My sister knew better and called the ambulance anyway, and they rushed me to Augusta medical center. After a series of x-rays, they discovered my pelvis was split totally in half into two pieces, leaving a three-quarter-inch canal running from top to bottom. Augusta medical center could not handle this severe an injury. They rushed me to University of Virginia medical center, where more x-rays were taken and eventually surgery. After a series of surgeries then and into the future, I would have three pins, two plates, and two total hip replacements necessary because of necrosis in the joints.

Adding to this, I have a lower disk bulge, thoracic issues, as well as degenerative arthritis in my knees, hips, shoulders, and hands. Many evenings and days I have been in pain. This has required a regimen of medication, working out, swimming, maintaining healthy eating habits, and a lot of prayer.

Some days I cannot even function, and those days nothing works. When the pain is unbearable, I want to die. It has often been a trigger for bipolar depression. Wanting to die, I have realized, is extremely selfish. It focuses only on my pain, not even considering God's plan or the impact on others. Challenged by this thought, I had an epiphany. Going back to a Scripture mentioned previously, I came to a realization that I could use Proverbs 3, which Dr. Brown told me when I was diagnosed with HIV, as a meditation and prayer to help me deal with the pain. Learning to use this has helped me deal with extreme cases of pain. The word of God is and always will be the important ingredient. When I work out and swim, I repeat prayers and Scriptures. The effects of this are amazing. God does not take *all* the pain away; however, He takes enough that I am able to do His will.

Every day is unpredictable regarding my physical pain. Waking up in the morning, I lay back and contemplate my relationship with God and what the events of the day may bring. In most cases, I awake with a refreshed body; however, in the background of my body, I can feel the undercurrent of pain that comes from stiff joints and the fallout from all the hard work I put my body through, as well as the surgeries. Sometimes the weather determines the level of pain.

The levels of pain I have can be combated by high doses of medication and a regimen of working out and stretches. Although I take medication and work out, the pain never completely goes away. Some days it is all I can do to deal with it. Taking medication works, but the side effects make me feel strange. Compounding the problem is my past drug addiction to opiates, the one type of pain medication that works to relieve my pain. More recently, I went through detox again to get off these medications completely. The level of pain has increased as a result, but God is helping me work through it. Pain is something I have had to accept. What I am finding works the best is focusing on God and His word. Recently God led me to John 5 where Jesus asks the paralyzed man by the pool if he wants to be made well, and the man has all sorts of excuses for not being healed. Jesus heals him and tells him to sin no more. I felt God was telling me to stop making excuses and get off the addicting pain meds. He is continuing to help me through His word.[1]

---

[1]   See John 5:2–14

> This is my comfort in my affliction, that your
> promise gives me life.
>
> It is good for me that I was afflicted, that I might
> learn your statutes. (Ps. 119:50, 71)

In a very good way, God has used my physical pain to draw me into a deeper relationship with Him. It is not that God wants me to be in pain, but He wants to put my faith and walk as a Christian into practice. I find peace when I can bring my pain to Him. I find joy when I bring my physical pain to Him and He uses it to bring me into oneness. I find encouragement when I bring my pain and the resulting depression to a close brother in Christ who reminds me of God's purposes in my life.

I have literally been broken, meaning many of my bones have had to undergo surgery to mend me back together. They have been mended together by titanium pins, plates, and artificial joints. In the area of pain, God didn't cause it, but He allowed it to break me, to show me that dependence on Him was needed all the more. Do not get me wrong, I am not saying that people who are in pain should not use the gifts God gave us, such as medications and doctors and praying for healing. I am merely saying, speaking for myself only, that God has used the pain in my body to break me and mold me into a deeper oneness with Him. You could say it is a process, of shedding the old and adding the new spiritually. My pain has transformed me to be more spiritual, leaning on God and reading and meditating on His word. Just as Jacob wrestled with God until God put his hip out of joint, and even then wouldn't let go until God had blessed him, so I too have wrestled with God, had my hips put out of joint, and yet received a great blessing![2] My pain has also helped me relate better to Jesus and the pain He suffered.

In God's scheme of things, His mending of me is not of metal but of things that have more strength. These are relational and spiritual. God is mending my heart, mind, and soul using my unceasing pain, as I let it focus me on Him. This is done so that His work is made complete, so that His work in me can bring glory to Him and oneness to others.

Resources to Contact for Help

> Disclaimer: Not all resources listed are necessarily Christian, nor can I vouch for their quality or contact info. Do your own research before contacting, but be safe in using a computer—search information cannot always be erased.

> Call 9-1-1 if you are in immediate danger.

> Our greatest need is a relationship with Jesus! Call 1-888-NEEDHIM (633-3446)

---

[2] See Genesis 32:22–32

Online lists of many types of hotlines: keepthefaith.com/page/crisis-help, yourcross.org/hotlines

Rest Ministries: 1-888-751-REST (7378) (chronic illness, chronic pain)

Watchman Fellowship: 1-817-277-0023 (chronic illness, chronic pain)

Suicide Hotline: 1-800-273-TALK (8255)

Focus on the Family: 1-800-AFAMILY (232-6459) or 1-855-771-HELP, focusonthefamily.com

Family Life Ministry: 1-800-FL-TODAY (358-6329), familylife.com

Billy Graham Association: 1-877-772-4559, billygraham.org

Grace Help Line 24 Hour Christian service 1-800-982-8032

The 700 Club Hotline 1-800-759-0700

18

Brokenness from Sexual Sin

Into Oneness through Obedience

THE YEAR WAS 1991. I was living at the graduate house, moving forward after graduating from the program. Attending AA and NA meetings was no longer required; however, I chose to still go. These meetings were a place where people who were in recovery would socialize. They were a place where I would try to find a lady to date.

Some have said I was handsome, not to boast, and I was always able to find dates. Also I was very forward when asking for a date. When my proposal for a date was accepted, I would wine and dine the lady at one of the romantic restaurants in Boston. My favorite was the Top of the Hub in the Prudential Building in Boston's Back Bay area.

Getting to the top of Boston's second tallest building takes a few minutes. When you arrive at the top you can see the dark sky speckled with stars through the glass windows, which circle the building. The top floor was made to move so you could see miles around both in and out of Boston. I did this frequently.

In each relationship, the time would come to tell my lady friend I had HIV. What followed in every case was her starting to slowly push me away but without really talking about it. This caused a great deal of hurt, and I ended up not bothering to date anymore. My jaded feelings caused me to isolate.

After six years of not dating, I felt led to search for women who were Christian and also had HIV, like me. I did this through dating sites on the Internet. Many searches were dead ends, but eventually I found a lady who was interesting, a lady claiming to be a Christian who also had HIV. I was excited. In my excitement, many emotions came to surface, but these only deceived my thoughts and adversely affected the choices I would make. Let me explain.

In my past, when God was not a part of my life, I used women. I used them for my own personal pleasure. This is not a part of God's plan. So my relationships were empty, meaningless, and fleeting. In most cases, they were one-night stands. If they lasted any longer, they eventually ended because the sex became flat, and I found someone else to fill my void and selfishness. After I became a Christian, God used my singleness to teach me how unique women are, and the special intricacies of their feelings, emotions, and thinking. I learned how women can be extremely special. I found myself wanting to have a real relationship.

Living in this world, everywhere you turn there are men and women having relationships. Relationships in dating, going to movies, dinner dates, as well as attending church. Seeing this caused me to *feel lonely*. Now that I was a Christian, I had the dream of having a real loving relationship with a woman. Not one fueled by sex or selfish desires, but one that was drawn out by God, including marriage, sacrifice, and understanding. For the longest time, I deeply wanted this, although I denied it. I thought how nice this would be, especially being blessed from God. In my search, I thought I had found the one, the one who would fill the void! Alas, it was not to be.

> My son, keep your father's commandment, and forsake not your mother's teaching. Bind them upon your heart always; tie them about your neck. When you walk, they will lead you; when you lie down, they will watch over you; and when you awake, they will talk with you. For the commandment is a lamp and the teaching a light, and the reproofs of discipline are the way of life, to preserve you from the evil woman, from the smooth tongue of the

adventuress. Do not desire her beauty in your heart, and do not let her capture you with her eyelashes; for a harlot may be hired for a loaf of bread, but an adulteress stalks a man's very life. (Prov. 6:20–26)

In corresponding with the young lady, she mentioned she was coming to the States. This was in February of 2000. She was Chinese-born, living in Australia. She explained to me she was a Christian and her parents were too. She related how her family was working with the underground Christian church in China. Apparently her living in Australia was a result of her having been an exchange student from China to Australia. Through a series of bad choices, she contracted HIV from an Australian citizen. She told me that, because the government had invited her as a visitor and granted her exchange student status, they felt liable for the actions of one of their citizens, who gave her HIV, and so they granted her citizenship.

Prior to her arrival, I made arrangements for her to stay with a Christian couple I knew. I also thought it would be appropriate for the couple and their children to accompany me when I picked her up at the airport. This would help avoid a situation that would cause either one of us to make a bad choice, as well as maintain accountability and purity. Coming from another country, I also thought she would be tired and uncomfortable, and possibly a little scared.

The day came for her arrival. It was later in the evening. My friend's family and I went to pick her up. When we got to the airport, she had already arrived. The stars and moon ruled the clear evening sky. In front of the small airport terminal stood a petite Chinese woman with long black hair. As she turned, I could see her pleasant smile. We walked over and greeted her, explaining how my friends were going to be her hosts during her stay. Although Chinese, she spoke English well. After a brief conversation, I suggested that she ride with my friend and family to their house. After some additional small talk there, I went home so she could rest after her long trip from Australia.

She had planned only a thirty-day visit, but what happened over the course of those thirty days I will never forget. Through a series of dates and suggestive comments from her, I would find myself choosing to break my vow to God of celibacy. During her stay, I was at first reluctant to date her. My business was doing well, and I had just added a building and plumbing company. I was very busy and did not really have time for a relationship, despite my hopes for romance. My work hours were long and my church activities called for my attention as well. I think I was also scared, because it was a long time since I had dated. Looking back, apparently God was speaking to me through my sense of apprehension.

Eventually I went on a date with her. At first there was small talk, but this progressed into us talking about how we got HIV. Our conversation moved on to our relationships with God. She told me that she accepted Christ after making some bad choices regarding her lifestyle and relationships. She also described to me how her parents had accepted Christ and had been working with the underground Chinese church.

After a few dates, I started to avoid her so I could take care of business. I would find out later this was not a good choice from her perspective! One day she came into my office asking why I was avoiding her. I told her that I had a business to run. At this she freaked out, grabbed me, and started yelling and hitting me! I should have known then that this relationship would not work. Feeling compassion, I consoled her and told her we would go out for dinner that evening.

The evening came around quickly. I made reservations at one of the nicest restaurants in Staunton, The Belle Grey. Leaving my office, I picked up the young lady for our date. What happened this evening would be the beginning of a four-year tailspin. After a bottle of wine and some suggestive comments from her, I found myself in bed with her. I am not going to blame her—I am responsible for my own choices, and I knew it was contrary to God's word prohibiting premarital sex.

> Let marriage be held in honor among all, and let the marriage bed be undefiled; for God will judge the immoral and adulterous. (Heb. 13:4)

I have been paying for my decision even to this day. As I mentioned before, in losing my celibacy, I came to know what types of romantic feelings come from truly intimate relations with a woman, something I had never felt before because of my drug abuse. As many women as I had slept with, I had never felt such overwhelming feelings. Having broken my vow to God, I found myself "in lust." Not understanding the feelings, and not adhering to the word of God in this matter, I fell into my old patterns. I was confused and out of my mind, but this time I had nothing to take, no drugs or alcohol to make the feelings go away. I was infatuated and now addicted to the sex. I would eventually chase this woman around the world from America, to China, to Australia, to Hawaii, and back. (One good thing that came of all this was an experience I had smuggling Bibles into China.) Eventually my lady friend and I stopped having sex, and tried just sleeping in the same bed. This does not work either. I felt like a wet loaf of bread. What I learned too was why God ordains marriage before sex, not the opposite. Sex is such a powerful bonding agent that it clouds and even precludes all other parts of the relationship, before they are properly developed. Waiting until marriage allows the spiritual, emotional, and social aspects of a relationship to develop in a godly, healthy way, until a forever commitment is made, at which point such a strong bonding agent as sex makes sense to launch the new family in a wonderful consummation.

But instead, our fall into immorality was the beginning of a terribly dysfunctional relationship. My infatuation would take me from my business as I traveled the globe with her. After one year and six months, we got married. During our relationship, I supported her family by sending them money via her, completely depleting my savings over the course of three years. She did not work, and I felt an obligation to support her as instructed by the Bible. I did this wholeheartedly.

My own family was reluctant to support me in this relationship, even after we got married. Some personal history was involved in this. Over a long period of time, I had catered to my mother. I spent time and money taking care of her needs. With my new romantic involvement, my mom became extremely jealous and non-supportive, even angry and hostile. My father, brother, and sister were also not supportive, going back to the pattern that had persisted since I was a child. Nothing had changed. I still could not do anything to please my family.

Somewhere, some time in all this I fell in love; I do not know exactly the place or time, but I did. I do not think she fell in love with me. Then one day she received a phone call. Her father had died. Parents are extremely important in Chinese culture, and she was devastated. She needed to go to China to get her mother and brother and then go to Australia to make arrangements to bury her father. In support, I went with her.

But soon I had to come back to take care of business, leaving her in Australia to console her mother. Trying to put myself in her shoes, I remembered how I felt when I lost my friend Lisa to AIDS. Losing a loved one releases a great wave of emotions that blind us and make life difficult. Out of compassion, I felt compelled to support her all the more. I paid for all her families' plane tickets to go from China to Australia and back, continuing to deplete my savings. But even in the storms of life, we are still obligated to maintain our commitments to God. During an incident of this nature, we are called on for our utmost. In this loss, I consoled her. But at the end, she chose not to return. I was going through a hard time keeping the business together while she was taking care of her family. She put me on the back burner. She did not know how much *I* also needed *her* support, though I tried to tell her. With my business failing, I began to fall apart. I finally told her I needed her to put me before her family and come back to Virginia. She assumed I was going to file bankruptcy, which I did not. As I fell off the wagon, I confessed to her I was using drugs. I thought she would understand, have compassion, and come back and help me. Instead she chose her family over me. As my business took a turn for the worse, she filed for divorce, broke her immigration agreement, and never came back.

After the divorce was filed, I took this whole relationship to the Lord, and for the longest time held my covenant with Him regarding the commitment in marriage. She has tried to influence me to come to Australia for the past seven years. I told her I would be willing to reconcile if she would meet with a pastor and his wife whom we both knew over there, and I could meet with my pastor, so that the two pastors could help counsel us long distance as we prayed for God's direction. In recent conversations, she revealed to me she was unwilling to do this because she does not go to church now. During a conversation in 2015, she told me she was really not a Christian when she met me. She said it was not until her father died that she accepted Christ. She also told me she had other relationships with men after her father died.

I loved this woman, and I would have remarried her. But it does not appear to be God's will, since she is unwilling to seek godly counseling or even go to church. Nevertheless, one thing that *is* His will is bringing me into oneness with Him and teaching me through what happened to love her and forgive her no matter what she chooses to do.

There are many young (and older) adults falling into the trap of sex before marriage these days, and many are choosing to cohabit before or instead of marrying. The fallout from these choices is devastating. Statistics show an astonishing 86 percent of couples who live together will either break up before marrying, or get divorced after marrying.[1] The flurry of emotions surrounding premarital sex causes confusion and misguided thoughts of what is love. It turns out that living in an *un*committed relationship

---

[1]   *Living Together: Myths, Risks & Answers*, by Mike and Harriet McManus, ©2008, page 69.

is *not* good preparation for a *committed* relationship, since couples basically practice withholding what they give to the relationship because "it might not last." Love is a commitment to follow God's guidelines in marriage and to *not* follow the lust of the flesh. God's word clearly designates marriage between a man and a woman as the only godly, legitimate context for sexual intimacy, expressly forbidding it in every other context.[2] Like fire in a fireplace, sex in marriage can be a romantic, warm, delightful bond between husband and wife, but outside of its proper context, it will burn the house down. As I experienced, the lust of the flesh is deceiving and fleeting, whereas obeying God's guidelines brings oneness with Him and each other.

Resources to Contact for Help

> Disclaimer: Not all resources listed are necessarily Christian, nor can I vouch for their quality or contact info. Do your own research before contacting, but be safe in using a computer—search information cannot always be erased.

> Call 9-1-1 if you are in immediate danger.

> Our greatest need is a relationship with Jesus! Call 1-888-NEEDHIM (633-3446)

---

[2] Genesis 1–2, Leviticus 18, Song of Solomon, Matthew 19, Romans 1, 1 Corinthians 6, Ephesians 5, Hebrews 13

Online lists of many types of hotlines: keepthefaith.com/page/crisis-help, yourcross.org/hotlines

Focus on the Family: 1-800-AFAMILY (232-6459) or 1-855-771-HELP, focusonthefamily.com

Family Life Ministry: 1-800-FL-TODAY (358-6329), familylife.com

Billy Graham Association: 1-877-772-4559, billygraham.org

Prodigals International: 1-866-910-9002, prodigalsinternational.org (sexual addictions, porn)

Grace Help Line 24 Hour Christian service 1-800-982-8032

The 700 Club Hotline 1-800-759-0700

19

Brokenness from Mental Problems

Into Oneness through Medication and Meditation

Both medication and meditation ended up being the path to oneness for my mental problems! Flying off into the horizon, I would journey like a leaf being blown by autumn winds, floating whatever direction the wind would take me. This is a good description of how bipolar disorder has worked in my life. From a very young age, I was subject to uncontrolled actions stemming from this mental disorder. I had an impulsive, unpredictable way about me according to my mother. She said I was the one in the neighborhood who would climb the highest tree, wander the furthest from home, and explore the darkest sewers. I had an obsession with the unknown. My friends knew me as the one who would do anything. I'll share an example.

The town of Quincy where I grew up was known for its old quarries. These quarries were very high and very deep. There were two that I had a special interest in. One was at Faxon Park, which was closer to the south side of Quincy where I lived in 1975. The other was on the west side. These quarries are where my bipolar thinking would start coming to the forefront. Bipolar disorder used to be called manic depression, because it has two phases: a manic phase in which one has amazing energy, and a depressive phase in which one has no energy and sleeps a lot. In the manic phase, you often engage in risky behavior because you have a feeling of invincibility, a "Superman" syndrome where nothing can hurt you, and nothing has any negative consequences. In many cases, the choices I made in my manic phases were purely from not thinking about consequences. My first experience jumping was at the south side. This quarry's high spot was eighty feet, and within a day or two of going to this one, I was jumping from that spot into the murky waters below.

This high point was not nearly as high as the spot in west Quincy, which tops out at 110 feet and 100 feet in other areas. Over the years, a number of kids have died from jumping into these quarries. My friend Michael and I would meet on days mostly when it was extremely hot. We would walk to the quarry in west Quincy to have some fun. We would grab a couple racks of beer and start to get crazy. By the end of the day, we would be jumping the one-hundred-foot jump called Patty. One day in 1980, something happened.

Climbing up to the other side of Patty, we hit Wall, our name for a jump of about seventy feet. Michael and I decided to jump together, and this we did. Throwing a rock down to break the water, we grabbed hands and jumped. Somehow I landed sideways and was knocked unconscious. I was fortunate that Michael was not knocked out, because he dragged me to the shoreline and made sure I was fine, consoling me. God used Michael to save me from drowning.

But what happened next was totally the result of my bipolar disorder. Since I did not die, I climbed Patty, the one-hundred-foot jump, and jumped with great success. I did this *right after* being knocked unconscious! I hope this gives you an idea of how my thought processes worked, or in this case, *didn't* work! My choices during the manic phase were to find things that were dangerous and act on them. The closer to death, the more exciting, and the more dangerous the experience, the more likely I was to engage in it. It was like kissing death. This went on even after my accepting Christ; however, God taught me to pray and think before acting. But sometimes, when my mania was at its peak, I would find myself wandering, in search of crazy.

Over the years as a Christian, I have had many battles with bipolar disorder. It was not until 2009 after much experimentation that my doctors finally prescribed medication that worked for me. Prior to me getting on medication, there would often be several days in a row that I would not sleep, followed by days that I would get extremely depressed and do nothing *but* sleep.

In a one-year period, I would have what I called cycles. These cycles would run three to four months. It would be like climbing a mountain to get to a cliff and then jumping. What I mean is my periods of mania would get higher and more dangerous. I would get to a point where my mind would be racing so fast that I would hear ringing in my ears, besides the racing thoughts. I would become Superman or the Hulk. In college, during the manic phase, I would work out starting at 4:00 a.m. at my home and end at the university gym at 7:00 a.m. This would be followed by attending classes, followed by studying till 8:00 p.m. In most cases, I would fall asleep, however, only to rise within two to four hours. Even after coming to Christ, it was during these manic phases that I would experience the most temptation toward dangerous or destructive behavior, such as wanting to get high or going to the city to challenge gang members!

After my manic phase rose to its peak, I would then jump the cliff, so to speak, and crash. Following this would come a period of hell—suicidal thoughts, deep pits of depression, paranoia, and sleeping. This would last for five to seven days. I was no fun for my friends during these times! After this I would rise, enjoy a longer period of fairly "normal" thinking, and the cycle would start over again. Bipolar disorder has been one of my utmost battles, because toward the top of the mountain peak, I was unpredictable, impulsive, and compulsive, and in many cases, I was not able to control these urges.

I talk about my experience with bipolar disorder, which at times was also combined with mild schizophrenia, because it helps explain some of the things that happened to me in my life, a mixture of the illusion of control and being delusional. These terms refer to conditions associated with these disorders. These mental problems and disorders deluded me about reality. I would struggle to maintain an illusion of control at times using negative things such as drugs, alcohol, illicit sex, or pornography (which are obvious failures in life), and at other times using supposedly positive things such as material comforts, possessions, or businesses (which are seen as successes in the world's eyes). But what was the difference, really? In the end, they both enabled my illusion of control and kept me far from God and His will. And my battle with psychological disorders, biological disorders, as well as demonic spirits continued.

The manic phases were also periods of elation and driving ambition. During two of these phases, I built three businesses. I had a grandiose delusion of being greater than

I was. In the following deep depressions, I had a paranoid delusion that people were scheming and out to get me, which drove me to isolate myself. I would have feelings of impending doom and strong suicidal urges. These feelings did not automatically go away when I became a born-again Christian, although God did ultimately provide me with the means to deal with them.

Before I became a Christian, thoughts of killing myself plagued me. Many times I acted on these feelings. Once I gave myself a lethal shot in hopes of a rush followed by death. On another occasion, I played chicken with a tractor trailer late at night on the highway. Quarry-jumping was merely one of the first types of dangerous, self-destructive behavior during which only the hand of God kept me alive. By the laws of probability, I should have died on numerous occasions.

As a Christian, I still have these thoughts sometimes, but God has enabled me not to act on them, except for one time when I broke out on drugs while suffering post-traumatic stress disorder. The difference is that *living for God* far outweighs the "living" of *this* world. The consequences of sin on my heart nearly killed me, but my heart being cleansed by the grace of God through Jesus Christ saved my life. In the Garden of Eden, the fruit of the knowledge of good and evil was eaten. Using merely human wisdom, I was unable to make sense of my life. Out of my brokenness, God gave me *His* wisdom.

Who is wise and understanding among you? By
his good conduct let him show his works in the
meekness of wisdom. But if you have bitter jealousy
and selfish ambition in your hearts, do not boast and
be false to the truth. This is not the wisdom that
comes down from above, but is earthly, unspiritual,
demonic. For where jealousy and selfish ambition
exist, there will be disorder and every vile practice.
But the wisdom from above is first pure, then
peaceable, gentle, open to reason, full of mercy and
good fruits, impartial and sincere. And a harvest of
righteousness is sown in peace by those who make
peace. (James 3:13–18)

My prescription for these struggles was to listen to the
Bible on CD, as well as the many Christian ministries on
the radio throughout the day and evening. During the pit
of my depression, I would leave the radio on to listen to
Christian music as well as late night sermons even when I
was sleeping. In the last several years, God also used doctors
to discover medication that helped. I feel confident in
saying that the absolute best choice I made during bipolar
cycles was to hold close to the word of God, which saved
my life, and take my meds!

Staying close to the word of God has been God's way of
conditioning me to persevere and be relentless and rigorous
in my relationship with Him. This has brought me into
oneness with my Father in heaven. To this day, I practice

this absolutely wonderful habit. I practice this even in my good cycles. It might seem silly to expect God's word to do me any good during the times I was asleep, but in my experience, it seemed to help lay deep the word of God in the renewing of my mind. Out of the brokenness of having bipolar and other mental problems, oneness has come to fruition from *meditation* on God's word though CDs and radio ministers, and *medication* from godly doctors who had patience to take the time needed to get it right!

Resources to Contact for Help

Disclaimer: Not all resources listed are necessarily Christian, nor can I vouch for their quality or contact info. Do your own research before contacting, but be safe in using a computer—search information cannot always be erased.

Call 9-1-1 if you are in immediate danger.

Our greatest need is a relationship with Jesus! Call 1-888-NEEDHIM (633-3446)

Online lists of many types of hotlines: keepthefaith. com/page/crisis-help, yourcross.org/hotlines

Focus on the Family: 1-800-AFAMILY (232-6459) or 1-855-771-HELP, focusonthefamily.com

Family Life Ministry: 1-800-FL-TODAY (358-6329), familylife.com

Billy Graham Association: 1-877-772-4559, billy graham.org

Grace Help Line 24 Hour Christian service 1-800-982-8032

The 700 Club Hotline 1-800-759-0700

SAFE (Self-Abuse Finally Ends): 1-800-DONT-CUT, (366-8288)

National Suicide Prevention Helpline 1-800-273-TALK (273-8255)

National Hopeline Network 1-800-SUICIDE (784-2433), hopeline.com

National Association of Anorexia Nervosa and Eating Disorders: 630-577-1330, 10 a.m. to 6 p.m. EST, Monday to Friday, anad.org

Dual Recovery Anonymous: draonline.org (both addiction and mental problems)

National Mental Health Assoc: 1-800-969-6642, nmha.org

20

Brokenness from Loss of All

Into Oneness through Surrender

DURING THE DETERIORATION of my relationship with my wife, I struggled to maintain my businesses. Between the financial drain of supporting her and the deception and problems caused by my business partner, eventually I would lose everything. In my denial, I could not see how my own choices were contributing to the problem. Denial was another thing I needed to be broken from. The deception of my partner's contracts and work caused money to be tied up during court cases. Since I was financing everything (payroll, supplies, accounts, and more) from my own pocket, this put a strain on my resources for both the electrical and building businesses. As I chased my wife around the world,

I gave too much control to my partner. But he neglected to pay many of the bills so that he could maintain his whopping paycheck.

Payroll in one week's time ranged from five to ten thousand dollars including taxes, with twenty-five employees and a fleet of five trucks. During my building the infrastructure of the businesses, I had maintained a great reputation among vendors and clients in the surrounding community. My word was good. One evening in the fall of 2003, I was sitting in my office reviewing accounts. I finally discovered what my partner was doing. After a series of failed meetings with him, I fired him. Now I was responsible for the many pending court cases as well as both businesses, which at the time had a load of work that needed to be finished.

Not able to focus as I had done in the past, I hired some men to help manage and complete past and present jobs. Again I was not careful enough about the character of the men I hired. One new partner did jobs on the side for himself with my clients using resources from my companies. Facing the pain of marital breakdown, legal difficulties, financial strain, and an overwhelming workload, while working physically hard, fourteen-hour days in between court appearances and trying to estimate and supervise all the work, I finally broke.

Broken, confused, and having lost connection with my past supports of church and friends during my globe-trotting, I started drinking, which eventually led back to the crack pipe. Slowly I started to give up. Digging into my credit (at that point still good), somehow I was able to finish all of the work to a high standard and even clean up all of the court cases against my businesses, only to lose myself in the pipe. My habit escalated, and I became paranoid and suicidal.

At the end, I found myself sitting in a hotel room ready to end my life. I had a pipe with enough coke in it to kill an elephant, but dying was not God's plan for me. Deep down inside I heard a voice, the voice of God. He spoke to me, saying, "I am the way out, I will save you." Beginning to sense my brokenness, I grabbed my cell phone and called an older pastor whom I admired, Charlie Lewis.

> Jesus said, "The thief comes only to steal and kill and destroy. I came that they may have life and have it abundantly." (John 10:10)

I explained my situation to Pastor Lewis. He told me to hang on and asked where I was. By God's grace I remembered the hotel and room. I gave the location, and within the hour, he arrived with an ambulance. Knocking on the door, they had to push in against the chair I had jammed under the doorknob. They found me lying wasted on the bed unconscious. The paramedics picked me up and strapped me on a gurney.

As they rolled me out of the room, I came to. I cried, "What happened!?" Rolling down the side of my cheeks were large tears. Who would want to have anything to do with me, especially God? I was still a loser. And who wants anything to do with a loser? Looking back, I see how much God did love me, not because of what I had done but because of who He is.

As my tears rolled down, Jesus wiped them from my eyes. Going to the hospital was just the beginning of a year that I would have to endure, until I was broken again. I searched for God to help clean me up.

Alerted by Pastor Lewis, my parents and brother met me at the hospital. It was not till the next day that they were able to talk to me and then take me home to my mom's place. Numb and sitting in the backseat on the way home, I looked out the window at the mountains rushing by. I saw the sky and felt the heat of the day, but what I felt the most was a sense of nothingness. After arriving at my mom's home, I lay down and fell into a deep sleep. This was interrupted by a phone call from my wife. As we spoke, I explained to her what happened, hoping for some compassion and support. Instead, she told me she was leaving me and filing for divorce, which took me into another tail spin. In a rage, I threw the phone against the wall and yelled at God, "Why me!"

When I finally got out of bed, I grabbed a bag of clothes, jumped in my car, and ran away. I ran all the way to Texas, where my cousin lived. In a crazed mind, the road trip took me to crack dealers and crack houses all along the trip there. I left my mark in every state. The three-day trip took me six days, and one-half of an eight ball of crack per day. God loves me!

I say that God loves me because I should have died during this trip many times, from my actions and also from the people I met, who were not exactly churchgoers. They were more like me the way I was before coming to Christ. I hung with the prostitute, the junkie, the felon, and the dealer. It was as if I had opened a door to my past. It was like I had never been sober.

Running away to Texas had its consequences—the additional strain to my businesses, and me losing my mind, setting the stage for me to lose everything. After working on a mission field in Mexico via Texas, and getting a little sobriety time, I decided to move back to Virginia. I decided I could solve my problems by finishing the house I had started.

My credit was still good, and I had access to two hundred thousand dollars from a loan I had signed before I left. In my thinking, this would be the cure all. The project was already in progress before I left, meaning I had set the footers. I had to build the house now. After coming home, I scheduled meetings with the financier to obtain the allocation schedule for the draw of money so I could build. The main ingredient I missed in this was God's will.

Pulling myself up by my boot straps once again, as I had done so many times before, I hired a couple of framers and started building the house. Also, during this time, I was landing other work! Wow, I said to myself, it is all going to come together. Wrong. I was able to build the house, put it under roof, and close it in. Then something terrible happened.

Blam! The truck lunged forward, slamming me against the red-brick wall. *Flop!* I went down in shock. Standing in front of my office with a new hire, an employee in one of my trucks had jumped the clutch, which sent the truck plunging into me. It pinned me in front of my office against a brick wall, breaking my pelvis into two pieces, with a three-fourth-inch canal running from top to bottom.

Pushing the truck off of me, I found myself tumbling to the ground in shock and extreme pain. My sister ran out asking if she should call an ambulance. In my shock, I told her no, I would be okay in a few minutes. Wrong!

Physically broken even after two major surgeries, I remained in mental shock long after the physical shock wore off. Wheeling myself around in a wheelchair and also using a walker, I drove and drove to keep the business together, only to find myself drugging again. After a three-day ride from Satan on the crack pipe, I threw in the towel when I discovered to my horror one morning that my urine was white like milk with large blobs of blood in it. Once again I called on God to help me. I realized I would never be able to overcome my past without His help.

Through all of this, I finally learned true surrender. I called my friend Charlie Winkelman in Pennsylvania and described my situation. He invited me to move in with him and his family while I healed. I moved to Pennsylvania with a determination to be a "bond servant" of Christ.

According to the Old Testament, servants were to serve seven years for their masters. After seven years, they would be released. However, if they loved their master and wished to continue as a servant, they could choose to become a bond servant, which meant they would continue to serve their master for life. If they chose to become a bond servant, they would place their earlobe against a tree and run an awl through it, to signify their choice. In the New Testament, the Apostle Paul often spoke of being "a bond servant of Christ," indicating a freely chosen, lifelong commitment to serve Him.

Through my experience of brokenness into oneness, I also was led to choose to be a bond servant of Christ. Let me share how I came to this decision. All through my life I "maintained control" using the skills and behaviors conditioned from my past. I depended on these conditioned skills and behaviors rather than on God. They became tools of my flesh, that is, my fallen human nature. As such, they helped me avoid God's will for my life.

But in reality, I was never really in control of anything, having only an illusion of control, as suggested earlier. I was using people, places, and things in my arsenal to try to control my surroundings. But I was simply deluding myself into *thinking* I was in control.

This arsenal was brought to my attention through my relationship with Christ. Within this arsenal were manipulation, lying, psychology, humanism, relativity, education, drugs, alcohol, and sex. The list could go on and on, but you get the point. As I served Christ, studied God's Word, prayed, and fellowshipped with other Christians, the Holy Spirit began to show me this arsenal and how I was using it to try to stay in control of everything. At first these were just fleeting insights. Then one day, God showed me through his word that He was actually calling me to be a bond servant, like the Apostle Paul, meaning total surrender.

Total surrender. Wow, I said to myself. This will be difficult. And it has been! But I really had no other choice. I could continue on as I had, trying to do everything in my own strength, using my own skills and coping mechanisms, and always ending up falling back into my addictions, on the road to death. Or I could surrender everything to Christ, depend on His strength alone, and follow His path to life. Clearly my own way was not working. When I moved to Pennsylvania, it was not just a geographical move. I also made the choice to surrender all and become a bond servant of Christ.

Of course, this also was a journey, not an instantaneous transformation. I discovered there are many levels of sanctity or holiness that one goes through in trying to be totally surrendered. The exciting part of this is the permeating sense of peace that comes from being a bond servant! Instead of feverishly trying to control everything, I could rest in Christ and follow His lead. This is an invitation He gives to everyone: "Come to me, all who labor and are heavy laden, and I will give you rest." He also gives other fruit of the Spirit: love, joy, patience, kindness, goodness, faithfulness, gentleness, and self-control. (See chapter 23 for more on the fruit of the Spirit.)

> Come to me, all who labor and are heavy laden, and I will give you rest. Take my yoke upon you, and learn from me; for I am gentle and lowly in heart, and you will find rest for your souls. For my yoke is easy, and my burden is light. (Matt. 11:28–30)

Total surrender is not easy to do. Once we take on Jesus' yoke, it is easy because He is yoked with us, like two oxen pulling a cart, and He does the heavy pulling! But surrendering and taking on His yoke in the first place is difficult. We are constantly tempted to try to control things ourselves. We find it difficult to really trust Jesus and let go. But who ever said that boot camp was going to be easy? This is just the next level, graduating into *God's* boot camp. Let me share some ways in which God taught me to surrender, take Christ's yoke, and be a bond servant.

When life seems unfair, it is easy to develop a spirit of contempt—for others, for God, and even for yourself. I certainly did this. But as I surrendered life's seeming unfairness to God, He asked me to learn to love, as outlined in His word. Being a bond servant requires us to listen and act on his word, putting it into practice. According to God, we must love, which starts with forgiving the ones who have treated us unfairly.

Another area of surrender is being accountable for our actions regarding relationships. After I slept with my ex-wife before we were married, I was called to be a man of Christ and own my actions regarding this, and not blame the other party. If I blamed the other party, then I would not be able to repent, because of my denial. Taking ownership of one's bad choices is a higher calling from God when we are His bond servant. This takes ongoing, repeated practice, from brokenness into oneness.

An additional high calling from God is having faith. This has been a hard one for me as well. The many physical, emotional, relational, financial, and spiritual conditions and situations of my life have been very challenging. God has called me to have faith regarding them. Some I have been able to give to Him with flying colors; however, others have been difficult to surrender.

HIV/AIDS was very hard to trust God with initially. However, as time has passed and He has shown Himself faithful in keeping me healthy, it has been easier to give over.

During my times of prosperity, it was easy to trust God with my finances. However, in the last ten years, this has been harder to relinquish. It was not until recently that I have been able to grow in faith and begin to surrender this to Him.

For example, over the past ten years, I have been given a Social Security disability allowance to live off by the government because of my injuries. This amounted to between $750 and $1,000 per month. This had to pay all my bills. Recently, for a time, I had a social work job, only to be fired because of my bipolar condition and a change in management above me. During my employment, I was able to save some money, but now my savings are slowly depleting. In addition to my bills, I have carried my debt from the failure of my businesses for eleven years. Believing God wants me to honor these obligations, I chose not to file bankruptcy, even though my disability would let me.

As I have trusted and surrendered, God has provided. He provided funds for college, for my living expenses, for paying off vendors, and even for helping support my daughter. At times I still feel overwhelmed. I am somewhat overwhelmed now, since the economy has led to a decline in jobs available for professional social workers (working with teenagers), and my condition of pain hinders full-time employment with any physical labor, which is required in my two professions as a master electrician and builder.

So what can I say? What I can say is what God told me: Be still and know that He is God and He is in control;

"Do not worry." Trust in Him and lean not on my own understanding, "HAVE FAITH"! It is easy to have faith when all around me is like a day at the beach, but much harder when I am at the end of my resources, in constant pain, with bills I can't pay, and the worry that HIV or hepatitis C will destroy my health.

> But I say, walk by the Spirit, and you will not gratify the desires of the flesh. For the desires of the flesh are against the Spirit, and the desires of the Spirit are against the flesh, for these are opposed to each other, to keep you from doing the things you want to do. But if you are led by the Spirit, you are not under the law. Now the works of the flesh are evident: sexual immorality, impurity, sensuality, idolatry, sorcery, enmity, strife, jealousy, fits of anger, rivalries, dissensions, divisions, envy, drunkenness, orgies, and things like these. I warn you, as I warned you before, that those who do such things will not inherit the kingdom of God. But the fruit of the Spirit is love, joy, peace, patience, kindness, goodness, faithfulness, gentleness, self-control; against such things there is no law. And those who belong to Christ Jesus have crucified the flesh with its passions and desires. (Gal. 5:16–24)

But God has taught me throughout my walk to have faith in Him, no matter what the circumstances may be. To put it in perspective, as seen by Him, he is King of ALL

THINGS, He is in control of ALL THINGS, He owns ALL THINGS, and what He has done, the good in my life and the life of others who have faith, He will keep doing.

My role is to have a growing and deep faith, love Him with all my heart and mind, trust Him, and continue to believe that He is in control, not me.

Through this journey, I am learning to become a bond servant. It has taken years of humility and brokenness, drawing me into oneness, becoming a true bond servant like the apostle Paul, and I'm not there yet. I still have a long ways to go, but I have faith in God that I am where I am supposed to be.

In his letter to the Philippians, Paul states that he has found the key to being content in all circumstances, good and bad; it is the realization that we can do all things through Christ who strengthens us.

> Not that I complain of want; for I have learned, in whatever state I am, to be content. I know how to be abased, and I know how to abound; in any and all circumstances I have learned the secret of facing plenty and hunger, abundance and want. I can do all things in [Christ] who strengthens me. (Phil. 4:11–13, RSV)

According to God, as we grow and mature in our faith in Christ, as we surrender our lives to Him and become His bond servants, the Holy Spirit produces more of His fruit in our lives and transforms us to be more and more like Jesus. He takes our brokenness and turns it into oneness with Him. The more I have surrendered to Christ, the more I have experienced his awesome peace in the midst of trials and tribulations. I am not saying I have always felt this way, but over the years, it has grown to be more and more. This has been my experience in my deepening walk with Christ, brokenness into oneness.

Resources to Contact for Help

Disclaimer: Not all resources listed are necessarily Christian, nor can I vouch for their quality or contact info. Do your own research before contacting, but be safe in using a computer—search information cannot always be erased.

Call 9-1-1 if you are in immediate danger.

Our greatest need is a relationship with Jesus! Call 1-888-NEEDHIM (633-3446)

Online lists of many types of hotlines: keepthefaith. com/page/crisis-help, yourcross.org/hotlines

Focus on the Family: 1-800-AFAMILY (232-6459) or 1-855-771-HELP, focusonthefamily.com

Family Life Ministry: 1-800-FL-TODAY (358-6329), familylife.com

Billy Graham Association: 1-877-772-4559, billy graham.org

Compass—Finances God's Way: 1-800-525-7000, compass1.org

Crown Financial Ministries: 1-800-722-1976, crown. org

Dave Ramsey solutions: daveramsey.com

Trinity Debt Management: 1-800-758-3844, trinity credit.org

Grace Help Line 24 Hour Christian service 1-800-982-8032

The 700 Club Hotline 1-800-759-0700

PART III

TRUTHS ABOUT ONENESS

As I have grown in my faith and ministry, God has taught me additional truths about oneness with Christ and why I have gone through all the trials in my life. In Part 3, I discuss the story of Joseph and God's bigger picture, embracing the fallout from my past, the fruit of the Spirit that has grown in the midst of my problems, the competing images from the world and God's word, how to deal with Satan's inevitable attacks, and how one can become and grow as a Christian.

21

Oneness and God's "Bigger Picture"

Why So Much Brokenness?

As I HAVE said, the fruit of God's grace through Jesus Christ in my life has been His transformation of my brokenness into oneness.

One might ask, why so much brokenness? Why did I have to go through so many trials and tribulations? Couldn't God have made me Jesus' disciple with much less pain and suffering? Some Christians seem not to have suffered as much and yet have a wonderful relationship with Christ. And others have suffered even more than me, with horrible diseases, disabilities, loss of children, injustice, oppression, and more! Why, Lord? Why so much suffering and brokenness?[1]

Through my life experiences, God has been revealing at least the beginning of an answer to this question. The full answer must wait for heaven, but a few things are clear.

Let me start with Scripture. The Scriptures that I share represent God's word coming to life in my personal walk with my Lord Jesus Christ, whom I have learned to love with all my being. My life is far from being like that of the Old Testament patriarch Joseph—it has been more like Samson's, one of continuous sin! But in the life of Joseph, we see oneness always follows brokenness that comes from evil. Let's take a journey, a journey back in time, back to the Old Testament, back to Genesis, the book of beginnings.

Joseph and God's Bigger Picture

The following story from the Old Testament book of Genesis provides an illustration of how and why God uses brokenness to produce oneness. (Explanatory notes are in brackets.)

---

[1] For an excellent, in depth treatment of this see Philip Yancey's book *Disappointment with God*.

Joseph's Dreams

Jacob [also known as Israel] lived in the land of his father's sojournings, in the land of Canaan. These are the generations of Jacob.

Joseph, being seventeen years old, was pasturing the flock with his brothers. He was a boy with the sons of Bilhah and Zilpah, his father's wives. And Joseph brought a bad report of them to their father. Now Israel loved Joseph more than any other of his sons, because he was the son of his old age. And he made him a robe of many colors. But when his brothers saw that their father loved him more than all his brothers, they hated him and could not speak peacefully to him.

Now Joseph had a dream, and when he told it to his brothers they hated him even more. He said to them, "Hear this dream that I have dreamed: Behold, we were binding sheaves in the field, and behold, my sheaf arose and stood upright. And behold, your sheaves gathered around it and bowed down to my sheaf." His brothers said to him, "Are you indeed to reign over us? Or are you indeed to rule over us?" So they hated him even more for his dreams and for his words.

Then he dreamed another dream and told it to his brothers and said, "Behold, I have dreamed another dream. Behold, the sun, the moon, and eleven stars were bowing down to me." But when he told it to his father and to his brothers, his father rebuked him and said to him, "What is this dream that you have dreamed? Shall I and your mother and your brothers indeed come to bow ourselves to the ground before you?" And his brothers were jealous of him, but his father kept the saying in mind.

Joseph Sold by His Brothers

Now his brothers went to pasture their father's flock near Shechem. And Israel said to Joseph, "Are not your brothers pasturing the flock at Shechem? Come, I will send you to them." And he said to him, "Here I am." So he said to him, "Go now, see if it is well with your brothers and with the flock, and bring me word." So he sent him from the Valley of Hebron, and he came to Shechem. And a man found him wandering in the fields. And the man asked him, "What are you seeking?" "I am seeking my brothers," he said. "Tell me, please, where they are pasturing the flock." And the man said, "They have gone away, for I heard them say, 'Let us go to Dothan.'" So Joseph went after his brothers and found them at Dothan.

They saw him from afar, and before he came near to them they conspired against him to kill him. They said to one another, "Here comes this dreamer. Come now, let us kill him and throw him into one of the pits. Then we will say that a fierce animal has devoured him, and we will see what will become of his dreams." But when Reuben heard it, he rescued him out of their hands, saying, "Let us not take his life." And Reuben said to them, "Shed no blood; throw him into this pit here in the wilderness, but do not lay a hand on him"—that he might rescue him out of their hand to restore him to his father. So when Joseph came to his brothers, they stripped him of his robe, the robe of many colors that he wore. And they took him and threw him into a pit. The pit was empty; there was no water in it.

Then they sat down to eat. And looking up they saw a caravan of Ishmaelites coming from Gilead, with their camels bearing gum, balm, and myrrh, on their way to carry it down to Egypt. Then Judah said to his brothers, "What profit is it if we kill our brother and conceal his blood? Come, let us sell him to the Ishmaelites, and let not our hand be upon him, for he is our brother, our own flesh." And his brothers listened to him. Then Midianite traders passed by. [*Ishmaelites* is a term that can refer to a collection of various tribes or desert tribes in general, in this case some Midianites.] And they drew Joseph up and lifted him out of the pit, and sold him to the Ishmaelites for twenty shekels of silver. They took Joseph to Egypt.

When Reuben returned to the pit and saw that Joseph was not in the pit, he tore his clothes [a sign of mourning] and returned to his brothers and said, "The boy is gone, and I, where shall I go?" Then they took Joseph's robe and slaughtered a goat and dipped the robe in the blood. And they sent the robe of many colors and brought it to their father and said, "This we have found; please identify whether it is your son's robe or not." And he identified it and said, "It is my son's robe. A fierce animal has devoured him. Joseph is without doubt torn to pieces." Then Jacob tore his garments and put sackcloth on his loins and mourned for his son many days. All his sons and all his daughters rose up to comfort him, but he refused to be comforted and said, "No, I shall go down to Sheol [the grave] to my son, mourning." Thus his father wept for him. Meanwhile the Midianites had sold him in Egypt to Potiphar, an officer of Pharaoh, the captain of the guard. (Gen. 37:1–36)

This is the beginning of a fifteen-year ordeal Joseph goes through, during which he journeys from brokenness into oneness.[2] When he arrives in Egypt, he is sold to an Egyptian official, whose wife tries unsuccessfully to seduce him and then falsely accuses him of attempted rape when he refuses her advances. Thrown in jail, Joseph has God with him in all he does, and is enabled to interpret accurately the prophetic dreams of two fellow prisoners, one of whom was Pharaoh's butler.

---

[2]   Parts of the following discussion are from an unpublished sermon, "God Meant It for Good" by Pastor Charlie Winkelman, © 2005, used by permission.

Then God gives Pharaoh a dream: a dream which none of his wise men or magicians can interpret. Pharaoh's butler remembers the Hebrew slave he met in prison, Joseph, who had interpreted his dream two years before. Joseph tells Pharaoh his dream is from God, informing him there will be seven years of plenty, followed by seven years of famine. Pharaoh makes Joseph his prime minister, in charge of saving up grain during the years of plenty to eat in the years of famine. God gives Joseph success in doing this. When famine comes to Canaan, Joseph's father, Jacob, sends his brothers to Egypt to buy grain from—you guessed it—their brother Joseph. But in his Egyptian makeup, they don't recognize him. Joseph puts his brothers through a series of ordeals, to test their character and change of heart. His brothers realize their guilt and pass the tests. All during this time, his brothers think they are simply buying grain from a demanding ruler. But there's a *bigger* picture!

The bigger picture is the ruler is their long-lost brother! The one they wanted to kill but sold into slavery is now prime minister of Egypt! When Joseph reveals himself to them, they are speechless with fear. All they can see is their guilt in what they did to him, and the revenge they dread he will take. But there's an even *bigger* picture.

Joseph immediately reassures them that they have nothing to fear from him, because God has used their actions to send him on to Egypt to preserve their lives. Three times he tells them it was not *they* but *God* who sent him there. The bigger picture is that God Himself is Sovereign—in control of all of history! How He controls that history to help us is called God's *providence*—His *providing* for us in every circumstance.

Who gave Joseph his personality and his dreams? God did! Who brought Midianite/Ishmaelite traders by at just right time? God did! Who gave Joseph success as a slave and prisoner? God did! Who gave dreams to Pharaoh's butler and Pharaoh, and the interpretation to Joseph? God did! Who brought seven good years then seven bad years to fulfill those dreams? God did! Who brought Joseph's brothers to Egypt and gave Joseph wisdom to know how to answer them? God did!

This is not just a nice story to encourage us to be faithful in trials. It does do that, but there is yet a *bigger* picture! This true story also reveals the power and sovereignty of GOD! He controls history for His own purpose. He can even use the evil that we freely choose to do, to accomplish His purposes! Joseph says to his brothers, "*You* intended it for evil, but *God* meant it for *good*!" That is the *bigger* picture!

Now, just because God can redeem evil does not mean that we should take sin lightly! The evil of sin is redeemed at great cost, both to ourselves, and ultimately to Jesus on the cross. God would much *rather* work through our obedience—but He is able to work to redeem even our sins, and the sins of all.

Romans 8:28 says, "God works *all* things to the good for those who love Him, who are called according to His purpose" (emphasis added). ALL things. So God used the evil intended by Joseph's brothers, to work the good of saving all their lives.

I do not claim that I am like Joseph, but in my walk with God, God had to refine me so I could mature, as He did with Joseph and other heroes of the Bible. Samson, whose life was more similar to mine, committed obvious sins to the day of his death. He was blinded and put in jail, but even he was drawn to do God's awesome will at his end. The stories of Joseph and Samson are stories of hope, hope for all, even when we fall into sin. By believing and receiving Jesus Christ as Savior and Lord, we enter into a life of experiencing God's grace from the beginning all the way to the end and beyond into a new beginning. Like Joseph, I had to go through many trials and tough times before I could see God's bigger picture. Writing this book has taken me back to many of those experiences. The good news is the pain of my past is more than offset by the joy of joining with God in His "bigger picture."

That bigger picture involved God helping me *embrace the fallout from my past* to teach me how to help others…

22

Oneness and Embracing the Fallout from My Past

And this is the judgment, that the light has come into the world, and men loved darkness rather than light, because their deeds were evil. For every one who does evil hates the light, and does not come to the light, lest his deeds should be exposed. (John 3:19–20, rsv)

This is the message we have heard from him and proclaim to you, that God is light, and in him is no darkness at all. If we say we have fellowship with him while we walk in darkness, we lie and do not practice the truth. But if we walk in the light, as he is in the light, we have fellowship with one another, and the blood of Jesus his Son cleanses us from all sin. If we say we have no sin, we deceive ourselves, and the truth is not in us. If we confess our sins, he is faithful and just to forgive us our sins and cleanse us from all unrighteousness. (1 John 1:5–9)

Fallout is a word used to describe the harmful radiation that "falls out" of the air after a nuclear explosion. The word has come to metaphorically describe the harmful aftereffects of negative life choices and events. As I'm sure is clear by now, there has been a great deal of fallout in my life from the bad choices I have made. In *dealing* with the fallout, I made even *more* bad choices, choices that bound me to an array of sins, which became my means of escape. Escape was how I dealt with my problems, but it was a deception, because it didn't really solve them. It also prevented me from coming to closure regarding the fallout, and this added to my negative actions and feelings.

When I accepted Christ, the Holy Spirit brought this to my attention, like a light shattering the blinding darkness of a deep cave. According to the gospel of John, sinful men, speaking of me, prefer to live in darkness. But through Christ, God breaks through the darkness in our hearts and brings to light what we are unable to see.

As I saw my sin and confessed it, I was enabled to embrace the fallout from my past, because God used it to show me His tremendous forgiveness. I and others had intended something for evil, but God meant it for good.

He redeemed and transformed the fallout into a powerful force for the love and Good News of Jesus Christ.

Although I accepted Christ, it has taken these twenty-some odd years for God to reveal additional sins of my heart through the shedding of His light. This I know will go on till the day I die. I have heard it said that if it took twenty years to go into the forest, it will take twenty years to come back out. This is often true. However, I no longer regret this time, because it is time that God uses to shed light on the many more areas I need to address so that I can give them over by bringing them to the foot of the cross. How can I give something over unless I know what it is?

Sitting in front of my TV or computer, I see advertisements that present an onslaught of prescriptions to use to run away from what ails me—a pill, a vacation, or something to buy. Many times I have fallen for the alluring attractiveness of these temporal things, things that my past conditioned me to want. But can these things really help me deal with the fallout from my past, or was I being tempted to trade one form of escape—drugs, alcohol, sex, food, etc.—for another?

I have learned that these prescriptions, whether it be a vacation (geographical cure), a new workout gadget, a new movie, a new video game, or tonics and health pills that will make me feel young again, are merely a replacement for the ways of escape I used before I became a Christian! I am not suggesting that any of these are necessarily bad in themselves.

But if I think they are going to ultimately take away or help me cope with the fallout and pain of my past, I am being deceived. These things can only bring temporary relief.

> Is anyone among you sick? Let him call for the elders of the church, and let them pray over him, anointing him with oil in the name of the Lord. And the prayer of faith will save the one who is sick, and the Lord will raise him up. And if he has committed sins, he will be forgiven. Therefore, confess your sins to one another and pray for one another, that you may be healed. The prayer of a righteous person has great power as it is working. (James 5:14–16)

According the word of God spoken through James, confessing my sins to my brothers and sisters and requesting their prayers helps me to repent, to which God responds by bringing healing from the suffering produced from the fallout of my past.

I have learned to practice this through participation in various twelve-step programs. Early in my recovery, I attended many AA (Alcoholics Anonymous) and NA (Narcotics Anonymous) meetings, as well as an eight-week program called AWOL (A Way Of Life) that uses twelve steps to bring about deep change in one's life. God gave me these twelve steps as a tool. Along with prayer and the Holy Spirit, the practical application of this tool helped me see unresolved sins, which enabled me to bring what was seen, these sins, to the cross.

The Twelve Steps of Alcoholics Anonymous®[3]

1. We admitted we were powerless over alcohol—that our lives had become unmanageable.

2. Came to believe that a Power greater than ourselves could restore us to sanity.

3. Made a decision to turn our will and our lives over to the care of God *as we understood Him.*

4. Made a searching and fearless moral inventory of ourselves.

5. Admitted to God, to ourselves, and to another human being the exact nature of our wrongs.

6. Were entirely ready to have God remove all these defects of character.

7. Humbly asked Him to remove our shortcomings.

8. Made a list of all persons we had harmed, and became willing to make amends to them all.

9. Made direct amends to such people wherever possible, except when to do so would injure them or others.

---

10. Continued to take personal inventory and when we were wrong promptly admitted it.

11. Sought through prayer and meditation to improve our conscious contact with God, *as we understood Him*, praying only for knowledge of His will for us and the power to carry that out.

12. Having had a spiritual awakening as the result of these Steps, we tried to carry this message to other alcoholics, and to practice these principles in all our affairs.

In these groups, whenever we reached steps 5, 6, and 7, many people became reluctant to open their hearts and dropped out of the group. These steps involve true repentance and willingness to change, which offend our pride. In my case, it was difficult to do as well. However, with rigorous digging, perseverance, and humility only by the grace of God, I have been practicing these. Through the prompting of the Holy Spirit, I have been able to be accountable to Christian brothers concerning the sins and behaviors of my heart over the years. Through God's revelation of my sins and His sanctification, and though bringing them to the cross in repentance, I have found myself able to freely talk about my sins with most people, without feeling guilty. But this took a process.

Through this process, I have been able to take ownership, embrace, and not run away from the fallout of the sins of my life. At the beginning of the process, I tended to condemn myself. Recently God gave me a key insight about this condemnation. For most of my life, I had condemned myself for my sins. But this meant taking on the role of judge, which is reserved for our Lord Jesus Christ. This was another deception that came from Satan. But God helped me come to a new understanding.

In January of 2010, I attended an early morning Bible study at Jersey Shore Presbyterian Church. The leader was my friend of twenty years, Charlie Winkelman. The Bible study group was studying and discussing the book of Romans. I had read through Romans on many occasions and even copied the whole book word for word on paper, without realizing the deeper truth that is found in Romans chapter 8. This occasion was different. God came down, and the Holy Spirit shed his light on my self-condemnation. I had a startling epiphany.

> There is therefore now no condemnation for those who are in Christ Jesus. For the law of the Spirit of life in Christ Jesus has set me free from the law of sin and death. For God has done what the law, weakened by the flesh, could not do: sending his own Son in the likeness of sinful flesh and for sin, he condemned sin in the flesh, in order that the just requirement of the law might be fulfilled in us, who walk not according to the flesh but according to the Spirit. For those who live according to the flesh set

their minds on the things of the flesh, but those who live according to the Spirit set their minds on the things of the Spirit. To set the mind on the flesh is death, but to set the mind on the Spirit is life and peace. For the mind that is set on the flesh is hostile to God; it does not submit to God's law, indeed it cannot; and those who are in the flesh cannot please God. But you are not in the flesh, you are in the Spirit, if in fact the Spirit of God dwells in you. (Rom. 8:1–9)

According to the letter written by the Apostle Paul, inspired by the Holy Spirit, "There is therefore now *no condemnation* for those who are in Christ Jesus" (emphasis added). I had never seen before that once I accepted Christ and repented of my sins, He forgave me so completely that I no longer have to dwell in the mire of my past, no longer have to condemn myself! King David said in Psalm 103, "As the heavens are high above the earth, so great is God's steadfast love toward those who fear Him; as far as the east is from the west, so far does He remove our transgressions from us." Such relief! This allowed me to fully embrace the fallout from my past and move forward under Jesus' easy yoke.

The Holy Spirit helped me deal with my past but also produced fruit for my future…

23

Oneness and the Fruit of the Spirit

The Fruit or Fruits?

WHILE I WAS preparing to write this chapter regarding the "fruit" of the Spirit, God spoke to me regarding the word *fruit*. According to the spelling in the Bible and my research of other translations, the word *fruit* is written as singular, followed by the singular verb *is*. How can this be, when there are more than one fruit listed?

> But the fruit of the Spirit is love, joy, peace, patience, kindness, goodness, faithfulness, gentleness, [and] self-control; against such things there is no law. (Gal. 5:22–23)

Scripture seems to list nine "fruits": love, joy, peace, etc. So why the singular? An exciting part of having a relationship with Jesus and reading His word is that He always has fresh new insights to share! As I experienced God transforming me and renewing my mind, He brought to my attention how His grouping is different—that if I experience *one* of the nine parts of the fruit of the Spirit, the others follow.

To my surprise I found out later that Bible scholars have commented on this as well, proposing that all these nine things *combined* are the singular "fruit" produced by the Holy Spirit in our lives. The Holy Spirit gives many different "gifts" that are unique to different individuals, but *every part* of this nine-fold "fruit" is for *all* who follow Christ!

Twenty-four years ago (1992) my good friends Charlie Winkelman, Steve Emery, and I met on Saturday mornings at Steve's house for an awesome Bible study. It was actually a lot more than a Bible study—it was an accountability group. The text we used to organize our study was Richard Foster's *Celebration of Discipline*, looking at the various spiritual disciplines of the Christian life (prayer, study, meditation, etc.)

Since I was a "baby" Christian and early into recovery, I was very confrontational—something I had learned at the halfway house. The premise to the curriculum taught at the house was based on recognizing character defects in behavior, intellect, and emotion and then confronting them, with spiritual discipline as an additional ingredient. I brought this with me as a tool to use with Charlie and Steve.

This was not a good idea. As I confronted Charlie and Steve about what I saw as their faults, they naturally responded in kind, producing some very spirited exchanges! We had a joke regarding these at the meeting. We described it as pulling out spiritual Uzis (the Israeli machine guns) to bring to surface one another's sins. Recognizing character defects in each other's behavior, intellect, emotions, and discipline, we would unleash a hail of criticisms, producing an impact as if the particular target had been riddled with spiritual bullets! We had agreed to not react defensively but try to learn from each other. But the weekly shootouts left us feeling pretty wounded! (Eventually this triggered each one of us to speak up and confess our own sins before they could be shot at!) Often the shooting was done more out of pride than out of any sense of helping.

This was far from being the "fruit" of the Spirit. After meeting a few times, these firefights drew out degrees of hostile behavior from all of us. Through the prompting of the Holy Spirit, we decided to change our approach. What He did was to introduce the ingredient of love. Looking back, I can see now how this changed everything. By empowering us to practice love, the Spirit also produced in us, at the same time, the fruit of joy, peace, patience, kindness, goodness, faithfulness, gentleness, and self-control.

How did this happen? It happened something like this: The attitude of *love* changed the meeting atmosphere from being full of fear (of being shot) to full of *joy*, because there was *peace* (not warfare)! By the Spirit's power, love made us be more *patient* and *kind* with each other. This produced the *goodness* of discovering and confessing our *own* sins, making us more *faithful* to God, more *gentle* to others who were also struggling, and more *self-controlled* in our behavior. The powerful presence of the Holy Spirit accompanied all these and therefore produced the fruit. After this we took our Uzis and put them away.

In hindsight, I now see the Spirit's "fruit" as being a singular act in our meetings. Just as the Father, Jesus, and the Holy Spirit are one, the "fruit" is one as well. As I have contemplated this, I see how through Jesus Christ I have learned to love, and how the brokenness of my thinking is being transformed into oneness with God. I see this action as it worked then and now. In the months following this discovery, during our meetings we experienced great insight, revelations, and enlightenment from these expressions of the Spirit's "fruit."

Jesus expressing his love by dying on the cross for my sins is teaching me and my friends these treasures and hidden secrets that accompany his love. God is not all about the perspective as seen by the world. As I have been coming into oneness with God, life experientially has become a paradox.

For example, when I *try* to change my thinking, emotions, or behavior, I cannot. When I *stop trying* and turn it over to God, He changes them! In God's perspective, *death*, that is, death to the world and to self, means dying and being born again, by which I receive *life*. Being *poor*, meaning poor in spirit as well as financially, I become *rich* in the things of God. God has used my *brokenness* to produce *oneness* with Himself, one day at a time and one season at a time.

> For everything there is a season, and a time for every matter under heaven: a time to be born, and a time to die; a time to plant, and a time to pluck up what is planted; a time to kill, and a time to heal; a time to break down, and a time to build up; a time to weep, and a time to laugh; a time to mourn, and a time to dance; a time to cast away stones, and a time to gather stones together; a time to embrace, and a time to refrain from embracing; a time to seek, and a time to lose; a time to keep, and a time to cast away; a time to rend, and a time to sew; a time to keep silence, and a time to speak; A time to love, and a time to hate; a time for war, and a time for peace. (Eccles. 3:1–8)

We never know what each day or season will bring. To the world, a day is twenty-four hours, and a season is spring, summer, fall, or winter. This is true for God as well, but the Apostle Peter in his Spirit-inspired letter writes, "Do not ignore this one fact, beloved, that with the Lord one day is as a thousand years, and a thousand years as one day." God sees seasons not just in nature but also in the activities appropriate for various times in our lives (Eccles. 3:1–8).

But let me explore more the fruit of love, and a season when I learned about oneness and love…

The Fruit of Love

It was August of 2008. Almost every year since 2005 I have enjoyed a trip to the beach at Surf City, New Jersey, where Charlie's wife, Laura, has family with a beach house. The time at the beach is a time of friends and family. The days are lazy and relaxing. The evenings are filled with playing bridge and a variety of other games, or pairing up in groups to enjoy a round of miniature golf. Laura, in many cases, has won a trophy! We group up for meals also, each group being responsible for one meal. But the highlight of the vacation for me is the beach.

Rising early in the morning from my bed, I can feel the cool ocean air rushing through my room. It brings to my nose many tantalizing smells that accompany the ocean environment. Going out to the kitchen, I look at the tide clock to see when low tide will be so I can plan my day (the surf is best at low tide).

Planning the day at the beach is pretty easy. The activities are bask in the sun on the warm white sand until well done, get up and run attacking the large waves, and then swim for awhile. In most cases, the water is cool and refreshing, and when my roasted body engages the refreshing water, my body immediately cools down and I get a chill up and down my spine. Repeat until time to walk back to the house for the next meal. Bake, run, swim, repeat, eat! Each day at the beach house brought forth great loving and friendly relationships as well.

This particular year, my trip home would bring with it the beginning of different days and a challenging season. While I was at Surf City, my daughter Erica called to say her grandmother was dying and she needed my support. Before going home to Pennsylvania, I decided to go to Quincy, Massachusetts, where Erica was living. She needed support, but what happened next would also bring forth great challenges regarding love. Through a series of events, Erica, at that time nineteen years old, was kicked out of her mom's place and thus had nowhere to live. After long discussions with her, advice from my friends and Pastor Karen Rydwanski, my daughter decided to move to Pennsylvania with me. This would challenge and put into practice my love for her.

Over the last few years, my relationship with my daughter has grown deeply. Since Erica and I had not had much interaction till her move, you can imagine the challenges. There was a great deal of brokenness into oneness in our relationship over the days and seasons as I experienced parenthood for what was really the first time, and with a teenager at that! After moving into my place, she and I began to butt heads. One day after I challenged her, she got in my face. Let me express I am physically a big man and she is a small woman. When this happened, I realized that I needed to stand down and put into practice God's love. Erica eventually moved out and lived on her own. However, this changed six months later, when she needed to move back with me.

When Erica moved back in, my love from my oneness with God was further tested. My daughter and I are a lot alike in that she has a strong will like mine. However, to my surprise, during these months, she no longer lunged in my face, though we still had a tendency to butt heads occasionally.

In most cases, our society sees butting heads as being negative. However, in the scheme and eyes of the Lord, this also can lead to the application of love. Let me share one experience. At Thanksgiving, my daughter and I took a trip to Virginia to spend the holiday with my father, mother, sister, and brother. We stayed at my mom's. Because of my own baggage dealing with my mom, it was difficult.

Amazingly my daughter stood up to the plate and loved on my mom. In recent years, my father and mother had experienced a great deal of loss. My father had an extreme accident for which he underwent four major surgeries to his brain. My mother was released from a job she held for twenty-two years, which caused her to see life in a depressed manner and become very negative in her outlook and treatment of others.

As a result, my mother was negative to both me and Erica during our stay. However, my daughter reacted to this with love! The love that God had shown to me, and enabled me to pass on to my daughter, was now being passed on by her to my mom!

To my delight and amazement, Erica loved on my mother in a way that was very Christ-like. She did this by telling her she loved her even though my mother expressed nothing but negative feelings. My daughter, by acting in love and saying to my mother she loved her, defused any head butting. What a great lesson I learned! Erica also acted in this manner with my dad. I saw how the "fruit" of joy, peace, patience, kindness, goodness, faithfulness, gentleness, and self-control accompanied this act of love, and brought oneness to their relationship. On the drive home, I reached out, grabbed her hand, and said, "I love you," and big tears rolled down her cheeks.

This lesson of love has been reinforced in my walk with Jesus Christ through other days and seasons, in relationships with friends, during trials and tribulations. Through Erica's action, I had seen the Christ-like, other-centered love that she exhibited, and in the process experienced God's love even more myself. After she moved back in with me, whenever we butted heads, God helped me put into practice what I had learned from her. This has helped us to grow deeper in our relationship, bringing to fruition the fruit of the Spirit. Love is best expressed and put into practice in the days and seasons, in parenthood and relationships, and during the trials and tribulations that may accompany them.

As the Spirit produces more of His love and fruit in our lives, we look less and less like the world and more and more like our Lord. It's all a matter of choosing oneness with the right image...

24

Oneness and the Right Image

Society has a particular image of what it means to be successful or even "blessed." This "right image" includes having a perfect family, a nice home with a two-car garage, a good education from an Ivy League college, and a professional career that pays well. The right image in the world's eyes also means being the right weight, having the perfect body, and looking good.

As I wait in the supermarket checkout line, I see magazines showing images of people who are extremely successful and perfect looking, who have "the right image." In contrast, there are images of other people who *used* to be successful both in their career and image, who have fallen apart and no longer have the right image. These people are shown as obese, broken, and lost—in other words, losers.

As individuals we are all influenced by this "right image" that society defines for us. Even gang members with tattoos, body piercings, and "alternative" hair and clothing styles are driven by a desire to have "the right image" as defined by their own group. And Christians, who ought to know better, will often spend more time deciding what to wear to a wedding than they spend actually praying for the couple's new marriage!

What is the right image, really? Is it contingent on how we feel others see us? Or the opinion of a given group at a given moment? As seen in the magazines, this is a sad state of affairs. To live up to society's "right image" is a daunting task if we see ourselves as viewed by other people. What is deceptive in the "right image search" is what fuels it. I fall into this deception myself, and it has a name: pride. According to CS Lewis, pride leads to every other vice; it is the complete anti-God state of mind. It is essentially competitive in the way the other vices are not, focusing on "having more than" and "being better than" others.[1] My pride makes me want to be seen as having "the right image." But is this what *God* wants?

You might think that God is not concerned at all with image. But in fact He *is*! Yet it is a very *different* kind of image from what the *world* promotes. God's word makes clear it is not what we *have* or how we *look* that makes us

---

[1] *Mere Christianity* by C.S. Lewis, ©1963, page 122.

who we are. In Genesis, the very first book of the Bible, it says that God created man (and woman) in His *own* image.

> Then God said, "Let us make man in our image, after our likeness…" So God created man in his own image, in the image of God he created him; male and female he created them. (Gen. 1:26–27)

Now the Bible says God is a spirit; He has no physical form that we can see. So to be made in God's image has nothing to do with our *appearance*. It has to do with the attributes we have and the role we play in the world. We were created to be *like God* in some significant ways. Like God we are creative, we know things, we can reason, and we have a moral nature—the ability to choose between right and wrong. We were given a role in this world to also *represent* God as His ambassadors, to have dominion (leadership) over His creation on His behalf. This is the *true* "Right Image" that we were created to have, that defines who we really are in God's sight.

> He [Jesus] is the image of the invisible God… For in him all the fullness of God was pleased to dwell. (Col. 1:15, 19)

> And we all, with unveiled face, beholding the glory of the Lord, are being changed into his likeness from one degree of glory to another; for this comes from the Lord who is the Spirit. (2 Cor. 3:18 RSV)

Unfortunately, this Right Image and original *oneness* with God was *broken* when Adam and Eve sinned, which separated us from God and set us on the road to hell. Ever since then, God has been moving in history to restore that Right Image in us, to restore our *oneness* with Himself! He sent His Son Jesus Christ as the perfect embodiment of His Right Image (see Colossians 1:15–19), and as the perfect sacrifice to pay for our sins through His death on the cross. When we trust in Jesus as our Lord and Savior, God begins restoring that Right Image in us, bit by bit, so that we more and more look like our Savior, not in appearance, but in character and love (2 Cor. 3:18).

So the question remains—the right image or the Right Image? As seen by God, the Right Image does not come from having a family, a nice home with a two-car garage, a good education from an Ivy League college, or a professional career that pays well. In the eyes of God, the Right Image also does not come from being the right weight, having the perfect body, and looking good. In God's view, the Right Image comes from having a personal relationship with Jesus Christ, not from what we have or how we look. As the Holy Spirit internalizes Christ's love within us and then outwardly expresses the "fruit" of the Spirit through us, He transforms us more and more into the likeness of Christ, the Right Image of God.

Speaking for myself, I have fallen into the trap of chasing the right image from the world's point of view, with great success in worldly terms, but great failure as seen by God. Not that God will not *use* the skills He has given me, which were a product of my endeavors in seeking the right image. God does not want me to condemn myself because of any feelings that I have from not being the *worldly* right image. What God wants me to do is see myself through the eyes of Jesus.

God loves all of us through His Son Jesus Christ. As we accept Him, He gives us His eternal perspective regarding the Right Image that He created us to have. But living in this world it is still easy for us to listen to the lies of Satan regarding the right image. Past rejection can fuel chasing that worldly right image if one is not careful. Satan will continue to fuel this if not confronted. He will plant the weeds of worldly concern about our possessions or looks, and try to convince us that God has rejected us, by pointing out what we lack, hurting our pride. We must battle Satan by bringing our pride to the cross, where it can be crucified, freeing us from chasing the world's right image.

It is to this battle with Satan that we now turn…

25

Oneness and Victory over Satan

JESUS CAME TO destroy the works of the devil, to seek and save those lost in Satan's kingdom of darkness, and He has passed that mission on to us.[1] Anyone who begins to heal from brokenness by growing into the oneness with Christ that I have been describing throughout the book will find himself or herself becoming a target for Satan's attacks.

Throughout the book, I have shared my experiences in life, through seasons that were both good and bad. In each season there were a great many battles—physical, mental, emotional, and spiritual. Although war or battles may seem bad, there is the victory that comes after the battle. Regarding spiritual warfare, God's daily victories in my

---

[1]   1 John 3:8, Luke 19:10, John 17:18

life have revealed truth and power that come from oneness with Him.

There are parallels from both modern and ancient warfare that provide perspective on this. Allow me to compare my Marine Corps boot camp preparation and conditioning with that of David as he sought to defeat Goliath in the ancient Middle East.

Modern Warfare

While in boot camp, the Marine Corps worked hard at conditioning and preparing us to endure the reality of battle. I remember well the few days of simulated battle I am about to share. Early in the morning, above my bed, I could hear my drill instructors screaming at the top of their lungs, "Get ready!" When you heard this, you knew that the next action was to get out of bed immediately and stand at attention on the line in front of our racks that extended from the back to the front of the squad bay.

The next scream was the command to get prepared. The following days would further stretch my physical, mental, and emotional being. After getting prepared in the squad bay, we were rushed out to the parade deck carrying seventy pounds of gear. It was still early morning, before sunrise. In the air I felt the hot humid breeze, causing drops of sweat to flow down my face like a dripping faucet. Accompanying this was the never-ending attack of sand fleas, which attached themselves to my face. We were not allowed to kill them; "they were our friends," according to our drill instructors. In the air I could smell the pungent odor of the swamp and sea, which comes along the coast at Paris Island, South Carolina.

This was the day of the forced march, followed by the experience of a simulated battle. After being forced to march for the next six to seven hours, over a distance of twenty miles, we came to our destination, the simulated battle ground. In the distance we could see the course, through which we would have to crawl in the scorching heat of the day. On the course there were barbed wired areas along with large bunker holes simulating the effects of bombs being dropped from above.

Around the perimeter were trees with moss hanging from them. It was as if they had long stringy hair reaching down from the tops, touching the ground. As the wind blew from the coast, the trees looked like they were alive, as they moved back and forth and the moss caught the wind like a sail.

There was no time to enjoy the beautiful nature scene. My focus was more on my thoughts and feelings—the fear of perhaps not being able to rise above this challenge. Starting from the beginning, our platoon was required to crawl on our backs and stomachs like crabs under the barbed wire to get from one point to another. In the bunkers, simulated bombs went off, and in the background you could hear the piercing noise of blank rounds being shot from AK-47s, the chosen weapon of the enemy, and our M-16s. With sweat pouring out of every pore and sand digging into my skin where it penetrated the openings of my clothing, I crawled, rolled, and scurried to make it to the end. Arriving, I rose from the sand pit, my heart beating like a drum and my emotions scattered about like bees buzzing from a busted hive, and moved forward to the next obstacles.

This involved walking through the forest on a recon during the day without being killed, surrounded by simulated battles. Many were "killed" so to speak, and me as well. It seems that on my recon I encountered a grenade and did not face the right direction, and therefore my head was blown off. (Some would say this would make no difference in my thinking ability!) And this was only a *simulated* battle. No way in my imagination could this compare with real battle as seen by the many veterans who have had the actual experience.

An Ancient Battle

Before talking about spiritual warfare, I would like to take us back in time to another place, a time three thousand years ago when the Marine Corps did not exist, a place in the Middle East, where a different kind of conditioning was being implemented.

Looking into the shadows of night, you can see a small figure sitting against a tree. Gazing into the depth of the sky is a young man playing a harp. It's as if he is the conductor of a great symphony of stars. As each note is struck, the stars seem to twinkle that much brighter in concert with his tunes.

This young man is David, and he is playing psalms to Almighty God. For many years, as a boy, David watched his father Jesse's flock of sheep while playing his harp and conducting the twinkling concert of the stars. He also cared for the sheep and defended them against attacks by wild animals. Eventually he was enlisted to soothe King Saul's spirit with his harp as the king suffered from attacks by a demonic evil spirit!

As time went on, there came a season of war between Israel and the Philistines to the West. The armies of the two nations were evenly matched. In ancient times, to reduce bloodshed, nations sometimes engaged in what was called single warrior combat. Each nation would put forth a champion, and the winner of their battle would bring victory for his whole nation. The Philistines challenged Israel to such a contest and put forth a champion named Goliath. (See 1 Samuel 17)

Goliath was a giant behemoth of a man, literally nine feet tall, with terrifying strength, wearing 125 pounds of body armor and wielding a spear and sword of tremendous weight. The army of Saul trembled in their sandals when they saw him. King Saul himself was a strong, tall, seasoned warrior, but he was no match for Goliath. Goliath, in his arrogance, mocked the Israelites as well as the God of their nation.

However, Israel did have a champion, though he was not seen as one, not having the "right image," not a giant of a man in size or strength, but a champion who was a mere boy. Yet he *was* a giant of a man in terms of his powerful oneness with God! With Goliath's taunts ringing in his ears, David cried out, "Who *is* this uncircumcised Philistine that he should defy the armies of the living God!" (1 Sam. 17:26).

Because of David's oneness with God, he fearlessly challenged Goliath. With no heavy armor or large sword, armed only with a shepherd's sling and five smooth stones, David went forward to meet the giant. Goliath mocked him, but David responded, "You come to me with sword, spear and javelin; but I come to you in the name of the Lord Almighty, the God of the armies of Israel, whom you have defied. This day the Lord will deliver you into my hand, and I will strike you down, and cut off your head; and I will give the dead bodies of the army of the Philistines this day to the birds of the air and to the wild beasts of the earth; that all the earth may know that there is a God in Israel, and that all this assembly may know that the Lord saves not with sword and spear; for the battle is the Lord's and He will give you into our hand" (1 Sam. 17:45–47).

With that, David placed a stone in his sling, ran toward Goliath, and slung the stone so tremendously that it penetrated deeply into Goliath's skull between his eyes and forehead! As the giant fell, David ran up, took Goliath's own sword, and cut off his head! The stunned Philistines fled for their lives before the armies of Israel!

David had no Marine Corps training, no great stature, and no imposing armor. He had killed lions and bears who were threatening his father's sheep, but his primary training was *spiritual!* He knew the battle was the Lord's, and he trusted God to give him victory. And so a shepherd boy became Israel's greatest warrior, who, as the next king, would defeat all of the enemies of Israel, because of his oneness with God!

Spiritual Warfare

Moving forward in time, the date is now 2010. Sitting in front of my TV and flipping through the channels, I stop, and on the screen I see two strong men fighting one another on a show that depicts mixed martial arts. Flipping through more channels, I stop at another show displaying the battle as seen by today's military. Armed with high-tech weapons and the latest in light-weight body armor, these men demonstrate the power of a modern army.

Opening my Bible after a night of spiritual warfare, I take the word of God to encompass my whole being and prepare and condition myself for a different sort of battle. A battle that cannot be seen on TV or with the human eye, but that can be felt in my inner most being. Since I became a born-again Christian, these seasons of spiritual warfare have come all too frequently in the spiritual arena with Satan.

The Bible says, "Cast all your anxieties on God, for He cares about you. Be sober, be watchful. Your adversary the devil prowls around like a roaring lion, seeking someone to devour. Resist him, firm in your faith, knowing that the same experience of suffering is required of your brotherhood throughout the world" (1 Pet. 5:7–9). According to the word of God, Satan prowls around like a roaring lion ready to devour me. This battle with Satan I cannot win by using any weapon that is of man. This battle can only be won by using the word of God. According to the Bible, we must put on the whole armor of God.

The Whole Armor of God

Finally, be strong in the Lord and in the strength of his might. Put on the whole armor of God that you may be able to stand against the schemes of the devil. For we do not wrestle against flesh and blood, but against the rulers, against the authorities, against the cosmic powers over this present darkness, against the spiritual forces of evil in the heavenly places. Therefore take up the whole armor of God, that you may be able to withstand in the evil day, and having done all, to stand firm. Stand therefore, having fastened on the belt of truth, and having put on the breastplate of righteousness, and, as shoes for your feet, having put on the readiness given by the gospel of peace. In all circumstances take up the shield of faith, with which you can extinguish all the flaming darts of the evil one; and take the helmet of salvation, and the sword of the Spirit, which is the word of God, praying at all times in the Spirit, with all prayer and supplication. To that end keep alert with all perseverance, making supplication for all the saints. (Eph. 6:10–18)

Throughout my Christian walk, I have experienced battles won by doing what God tells us in Ephesians 6. But we must not *underestimate* the power of Satan. The battles that have been won have not been won alone. In addition to God's word, I have learned that I must take into battle with me other warriors, especially Christian friends who know the reality of Satan's attacks, who are faithful in prayer, and who are willing to be honest and help keep me accountable by speaking God's word into my life. I have also been helped by many of the preachers on Christian Radio.

Satan knows me and other Christians well. He and his demons know our weaknesses and common temptations. For example, Satan will not plant in my mind to rob a bank, because that is not something I have done or been tempted to do. Instead, he will tempt me with sins from my past, temptations I've given in to before, whispering in my ear that I'm bound to give in again just as I have in the past.

These satanic attacks bring the *opposite* of the fruit of the Spirit, i.e. apathy, depression, hatred, impatience, cruelty, evil thoughts, betrayal, harshness, and impulsive acting out, not to mention the "works of the flesh" that Paul lists: sexual immorality, impurity, sensuality, idolatry, sorcery, enmity, strife, jealousy, fits of anger, selfishness, dissensions, divisions, envy, drunkenness, orgies, and the like.[2] In my own life he specializes in hate, anger, disbelief, and contempt toward the world as well as the people who once harmed me, which is the product of my past. These are powerful weapons, especially when I try to face him alone. But they are no match for the power of the Holy Spirit activated by prayer! Satan was defeated at the cross by Jesus Christ, as prophesied all the way back in Genesis 3 and finally consummated in the end times revealed in Matthew 24 and the whole book of Revelation.

If we are tuned in to the Spirit, we can see the ploys of Satan in society. One ploy that I recognized during my education was in the battleground of ambiguity. In this battleground, Satan plants the seed that "there are no absolutes and everything is relative." This is a big lie, which I experienced both as a non-Christian and a Christian. Relativity sets up a victim mentality where I can blame my sin on everything but me. One gift of the Spirit we all ought to pray for is the gift of discernment, which helps us know which influences are from Satan or his demons,

---

[2] Galatians 5:19–21

and which are from God. This gift is also helped by a solid knowledge and memorization of God's word, which the Holy Spirit can bring to mind at the right time.

The condition of our hearts being vulnerable and prone to satanic temptation and sin has been with humankind since the choices made in the Garden of Eden. Our fallenness and depravity as human beings is an absolute in life. Whoever does *not* choose to believe and receive the grace freely given through the death and resurrection of Jesus Christ by accepting Him as Savior and Lord will surely go to hell in payment for their sins, which is Satan's ultimate goal for us.

But that is *not God's* goal for us! Satan is a liar and the father of lies, a thief, who comes to steal, kill, and destroy. But Jesus Christ is the Good Shepherd who came to lay down His life for us sheep so that we might have life, and have it abundantly, and eternally! Once we receive Him, He never lets us go![3]

Satan is real, he is subtle and deceptive, and he wants to take you down. *Far* down. But Jesus has defeated him, and wants to give you eternal life, as well as daily victory over Satan, through oneness with God.

Would you like to experience that victory and receive that eternal life? You can, by believing and receiving Jesus as your Savior and Lord. Turn now to the next chapter to find out how!

---

[3]   John 10:10–11, 27–29

26

Oneness and Becoming a Christian

How to Have Oneness with God, and Eternal Life

WOULD YOU LIKE to experience moving from brokenness into oneness with God, from spiritual death into eternal life? You can, by believing and receiving Jesus as your Savior and Lord. When you do that, you will be born again spiritually, filled with the Holy Spirit, started on your journey from brokenness into oneness with God, and guaranteed a home in heaven! And you can do that today, right *now*! Here's how:

How to Be Saved

The Bible says that God so loved the world that He gave His only Son, that whoever believes in Him should not perish but have eternal life (John 3:16).

All have sinned—you, me, everybody—and fallen short of the glory of God (Rom. 3:23). The wages (or result) of sin is death (eternal separation from God in hell), but the free gift of God is eternal life in Christ Jesus our Lord (Rom. 6:23).

God shows His love for us in that while we were yet sinners, Christ died for us (Rom. 5:8). God is just and must punish sin. But Jesus took the death penalty for our sin, on the cross, to reconcile us to God and give us eternal life.

If you confess with your lips that Jesus is Lord and believe in your heart that God raised Him from the dead, you will be saved (Rom. 10:9). For "everyone who calls upon the name of the Lord will be saved" (Rom. 10:13). Jesus came to His own home, and His own people did not receive Him. But to all who received Him, who believed in His name, He gave power to become children of God, who were born, not of the will of the flesh nor of the will of man, but of God (John 1:11–13).

You can believe and receive Jesus as your Savior and Lord through prayer, such as the following (choose to believe this in your heart and pray it with faith, trusting in Jesus):

Dear Jesus, I know I am a sinner who deserves death. I believe you died for my sins on the cross and rose again from the dead. I turn away from my sins and invite you now to come into my heart as my Savior and Lord. I trust in you and surrender my life to you. Help me follow you. Thank you for saving me! Amen.

If you just prayed for the first time to receive Jesus as your Savior and Lord, first let me say, Welcome to the family! I am now your brother in Christ, and we will spend eternity together with our Savior! OORAH! Did you know the angels in heaven are now throwing a party over you? Jesus says there is more joy in heaven over one sinner who repents than over ninety-nine righteous persons who need no repentance! I praise God that you have joined God's family! I want to encourage you to do some things that will help you in your new walk with Christ:

1. Find a church that preaches the Bible and the Good News about Jesus Christ. Worship there weekly and get involved in their activities for new believers. A small group Bible study is an especially good activity. Help support the church by giving to it generously each week.

2. Get a Bible and read it daily, beginning with the Gospel of John. Pick a place and time to read each day. There are different translations of Bibles—find one you can understand, perhaps with study

notes to help explain details. The English Standard Version (ESV), New International Version (NIV), and New Living Translation (NLT) are some of the good versions to choose from, and the Life Application Bible (in various versions) has excellent study notes to help you apply God's Word in your life. The website christianbook.com has great selection and discounts if you need to buy a Bible, or try your local Christian bookstore.

3. Pray every day—just talk to God, praising and thanking Him for who He is and what He has done, confessing to Him things you've done wrong, and asking Him for things you need. The Lord's Prayer in Matthew 6:9–13 can also give you some ideas about what to pray.

4. Tell others about your new faith in Christ! Jesus has saved you—that's Good News that you can share with other people who are lost, broken, or hurting!

5. Write me to tell me about your decision! I want to celebrate with you and send you some free materials. E-mail me at ericwong8238@gmail.com.

If you did *not* pray to receive Jesus and have never done so, I encourage you to pray asking God to help you take this crucial step of faith! If you have questions and want to talk to somebody about this, I urge you to call 1-888-NEEDHIM (1-888-633-3446).

But *don't put off taking this step!* None of us knows what will happen tomorrow, and once you die, it is *too late* to give your life to Jesus. If you've read this far, the Holy Spirit is speaking to your heart! Why not trust and receive Jesus *today*, and be assured that you will receive the blessing of brokenness into oneness in *this* life and in the *life to come* a guaranteed place in heaven, which Jesus Himself is preparing for you!

Serendipity

Early in my recovery and Christianity, I would take trips to New Hampshire to climb Mount Lafayette. Mount Lafayette is located in Franconia Notch and rises 5,260 feet above sea level. It is a strenuous climb. At one point on the trail, there is an overview, a point of rest. At this overview, I would yell out and hear the echo of my voice. This echo reminds me of how God has spoken to me through many serendipitous experiences. The dictionary defines *serendipity* as the accidental discovery of something pleasant, valuable, or useful. For me it has been surprising but never accidental!

Over the years God has echoed His commands using many people during my strenuous climb of life. In any given month, I would hear the same Scripture verse being spoken to me from two or three different people, on the radio, in books, etc. When I was diagnosed with HIV, I heard Proverbs 3:5–8 (Trust in the Lord…it will be healing…) being spoken to me by many people. Another time was when I was crushed by the truck and had to undergo separation from my profession and business. I did not know what to do, so God spoke to me Psalm 46:10 ("Be still, and know that I am God").

These are just a few. There are many more, and recently God has directed my lessons at church teaching the youth Bible study in serendipity. As I have climbed the steep mountain of life, I have found times after praying I would hear the echoes of God's word through serendipity and oneness. Perhaps He will speak in the same way to you! Be watching and listening!

Conclusion

Brokenness into Oneness has been a lifelong as well as daily experience, bringing me into an all-encompassing relationship that can never be broken. Being *broken* of my prideful human spirit was the premise for me accepting Christ as my Lord and Savior and experiencing an unbroken relationship of *oneness* with Him. I love Jesus with all my heart, and it is not by anything *I* have done or *my* love for *Him*, but all of how much *He* has loved *me* in spite of and in the midst of my sins.

> As [Jesus] passed by, he saw a man blind from birth.
> And his disciples asked him, "Rabbi, who sinned,
> this man or his parents, that he was born blind?"

> Jesus answered, "It was not that this man sinned, or his parents, but that the works of God might be displayed in him." (John 9:1–3)

In spite of the adversity and suffering in my life, the often empty "successes" and desperate failures, looking back I would not change a thing! Had I not experienced the things written in this book and God's redemptive actions in each area, I would not know how to love as Jesus wants me to love. With all my heart, my hope and desire is that God uses this book to show that it is not *who* you are as the *world* sees you, nor even how you see yourself, but how *God* sees you through his Son Jesus that really matters. Like the man born blind, the important thing is not the problems we face and why they happened, but the fact that God wants to redeem them and display His wonderful works in us!

This book is written for all—the rich, the poor, the diseased, the abused, the abandoned, the addict, the successful, the failure, and the sinner—all who have fallen short. God's plan for me and all of us is simple: fall to our knees, ask Him for forgiveness, trust Jesus as our Savior, receive Him as our Lord, and serve God as His children by reaching out to love others and spread the Good News of His salvation. I hope you will share this message (and this book!) with others who need to hear this.

> They shall hunger no more, neither thirst anymore; the sun shall not strike them, nor any scorching heat. For the Lamb in the midst of the throne will

> be their shepherd, and he will guide them to springs
> of living water; and God will wipe away every tear
> from their eyes. (Rev. 7:16–17)

Strolling down the aisles in bookstores, I have seen many books on acquiring happiness—happiness through meditation, through psychology, through working out, through proper dieting, through pleasurable vacations, through medications—the list goes on and on! Billy Graham reflected: "Someone has said that Americans… write more books on how to be happy than any other country."[1] This book, as you have seen, is *not* a book about finding happiness. It is about *overcoming brokenness* by becoming *one with God* and attaining *eternal life* through Jesus! Ironically, it turns out that God has designed life in such a way that oneness with Him is the *only* thing that will make us truly happy!

We see this supremely in the life of Jesus Christ, God the Son. His life actually sums up the theme of this book in a way that far surpasses the words I have shared. Though Jesus was and is God Himself, He emptied Himself and experienced the ultimate brokenness, on the cross, where our sin separated Him from any sense of His Father's presence, and He cried out, "My God, my God, why have you forsaken me?" Yet for the joy that was set before Him,

---

[1] From *Hope for the Troubled Heart* in *The Enduring Classics of Billy Graham*, by Billy Graham, as quoted in books.google.com

He endured this brokenness, this ultimate pain, to save you and me, so that we might be one with Him forever.[2]

Epilogue

Thank you for taking this journey with me from brokenness into oneness through the grace of God as He has applied it to my life. I would love to hear from you how it has affected your life or the life of a loved one. You can e-mail me at ericwong8238@gmail.com. May God richly bless you and yours in your own journey from brokenness into oneness.

In Christ's love,
Eric Wong

It has been a privilege and honor to work with Eric in telling his amazing story of God's love and grace in his life through Jesus. As a pastor, I have counseled many people who had some of the same brokenness that Eric experienced, but never all of those challenges in the life of just one person! We hope and pray this book will help you or someone you love to be drawn closer to the *only* One who can turn your brokenness into oneness, our Lord and Savior, Jesus Christ!

In His love,
Charlie Winkelman

---

[2]   See Matthew 27:46 and Hebrews 12:1–2.

CPSIA information can be obtained at www.ICGtesting.com
Printed in the USA
BVOW01s0851180816

459371BV00004B/5/P